COUNTY   GE

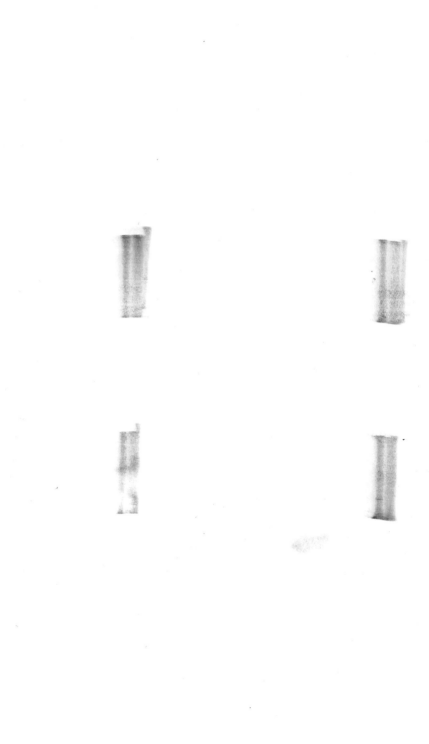

THEY FOUND TREASURE

They Found Treasure

Robert F. Burgess

ILLUSTRATED WITH CHARTS
AND PHOTOGRAPHS

Dodd, Mead & Company
New York

1   2   3   4   5   6   7   8   9   10

Library of Congress Cataloging in Publication Data

Burgess, Robert Forrest.
    They found treasure.

    Includes index.
    CONTENTS: Art McKee.—Kip Wagner.—Mel Fisher.
[etc.]
    1. Treasure-trove.   2. Adventure and adven-
turers.   I. Title.
G525.B8684   910'.453   77-1891
ISBN 0-396-07450-2

"Some may be tall, some may be short, some may be quiet, some may be voluble, but the first characteristic that all treasure hunters have, is an obsession."
—BLETH MCHALEY OF TREASURE SALVORS, INC.

"There is no way of getting away from a treasure . . . once it fastens itself upon our mind."
—JOSEPH CONRAD

Foreword

What is a professional treasure hunter really like? How does one get started? How and where does he find treasure? What makes him successful? In such a financially hazardous profession, what are his secrets of survival? Is it an occupation the average person can realistically aspire to?

These are some of the questions asked in this book. And who better to answer them than some of the most successful treasure hunters in the world? As you meet them on these pages, you will begin to see an interesting portrait of the typical treasure hunter emerge, a man of many talents, a man with a many-faceted personality. Although treasure hunters do not look alike, you will soon realize that they all have certain common denominators in their character, similarities that may make them quite different from you or me. Perhaps you will be surprised to learn that, contrary to popular opinion, even successful treasure hunters do not live happily ever after on the fruits of their finds, and unlike the storybook tales of easy riches, their lives are often one endlessly monotonous search for some small part of a nebulous fortune which, if found, may not even pay their expenses. So why do they continue? They tell you why, these adventurers, scholars, gamblers, businessmen, and sometimes rogues. And you will also learn how these gentlemen who possess such uncanny expertise in the fine art of professional survival do survive.

Occasionally you may find a treasure hunter's stories hard to believe, but let me assure you that for the most part they are true. After all, treasure hunters are living tall tales, and slight exaggerations are just another part of their lives. They believe them, and so should we. If a man tells me that he found thousands of dollars worth of treasure a week and I know the official records show he recovered little coinage but lots of historical artifacts, who am I to say nay? History has no price. At Florida's Division of Archives and History, the lead bilge pump that treasure hunter Tom Gurr recovered from the *San José* may be the only 1733 lead bilge pump in existence. Worth a fortune to a collector or museum? Perhaps, but to Tom Gurr it is still only a lead bilge pump that failed to bail him out of his financial difficulties when he needed it the most.

Also, as you progress through these stories and interviews, notice how the treasure hunters change. At first they search for treasure for financial gain. Then they gradually develop an interest in the history behind the artifacts they find. While one coin looks pretty much like another and these are needed to finance the hunt, the treasure hunter's real pleasure comes from finding artifacts of a more personal nature—a gold ring bearing a lover's message, a military medal traceable through a colorful history to a renowned soldier, an exquisite piece of Chinese porcelain with a fascinating story behind how it got where it was found and the wonder of its surviving centuries of destruction.

And perhaps this is what it is all coming to. Treasure hunting is no longer a solitary business. Governments are increasingly involving themselves in these ventures. The once colorful, inventive, independent treasure hunter of old is gradually being replaced by an updated model, the hunter of another kind of treasure, the history hunter, the underwater archaeologist.

In any event they are all here, each telling his story—how it was, how it is.

Robert F. Burgess

CONTENTS

THEY FOUND TREASURE

*At his treasure museum on Plantation Key, Art McKee reassembled
the scattered ballast rock, ribs and iron cannon of an early shipwreck.
McKee's early Florida treasure-hunting exploits make him the father
of Florida treasure hunters.* (Courtesy Florida News Bureau)

1 ~~~

Art McKee: The Treasure Hunter's Treasure Hunter

In a coral and concrete fortress lives my friend Art McKee, surrounded by his treasure, all of it under lock and key or in thief-proof vaults, of course. The fortress is a museum he built to house his finds on Florida's Plantation Key. The real treasure, however, is the man himself. A youthful sixty-five, Art is generally known as the father of treasure hunting, a tag he doesn't mind too much, just so no one calls him the grandfather of treasure hunting.

Actually, shipwreck treasure hunting is such a young profession, that it hardly got started until well into the 1950s after scuba gear became more widely available. Then, anyone with the price of an Aqua-Lung could launch himself into the deep and call himself a treasure hunter, as many did. And not too surprisingly, some found treasure.

But McKee was ahead of the crowd. He was the inspiration of our youth, the man who did it while we daydreamed about doing it. McKee was actively diving in the pre-scuba years of the 1930s and 1940s, when the only gear available was the hard-hat helmet and hose rigs commonly used then by commercial divers. In those years the number of men who had actually found and recovered sunken treasure could be counted on the fingers of one hand. Not only was Art one of these early pioneers, but over the years he made his treasure pay for itself in more ways than one. While most of his contemporaries cashed in their coins and gradually faded into obscurity, Art endured, keeping much of his treasure intact while at the same time learning how to stay actively engaged in new self-supporting treasure hunting ventures, a trade secret he reveals to us here for the first time.

On the day of the interview, McKee's museum was closed. But rather than disappoint a young couple that had stopped by thinking it open, Art invited them in and personally gave them the grand tour, *gratis*. As we moved from one display to another, Art reeled off, with the flawless perfection of a documentary soundtrack, the history of the Spanish treasure fleets and his recovery of some of their treasure, occasionally injecting witty McKeeisms that are as much a part of the man as his white hair and infectious laughter.

When the couple left, Art pulled out a couple of straight back chairs, and, in the welcome cool of the concrete fortress, surrounded by displays of diving helmets, old ordinance, clumps of coral and coins, bits of shipwrecks, treasure charts, salt-encrusted artifacts, yellowed newspaper clippings, and the unique aura that always surrounds sunken treasure, we started an interview that was intended to take no more than an hour of the man's time.

Five hours later it was still in full swing. Art and I were having such a fine time reliving his adventures that I was ready to pack my seabag and snorkel and ship out with him on a moment's notice!

Here, then, are a few highlights of those delightful hours. Picture the scene if you can. It is two o'clock on a balmy March afternoon in the Florida Keys. Outside the door, palm fronds rustle in the gentle ocean breeze. Wearing blue trousers and an open-neck white shirt, Art sits comfortably in the chair facing me.

Deeply tanned, his copper-highlighted white hair receding at the temples, he talks animatedly, punctuating his words with occasional laughter, recalling names and dates with remarkable ease and accuracy. His voice has the ring of sincerity. Throughout the long interview he toys with a small green Key lime. He starts by telling me that he was born in Bridgetown, New Jersey, on November 2, 1910 . . .

I attended high school up there and that was the extent of my schooling. After that I went to school with the fish, schools of fish.

I liked being outdoors. I used to go up in the deer woods or down in the swamps, just wandering around. I got a canoe and would take it up to the head of a stream and then follow it all the way back down to the lake. I went down the river and then paddled across Delaware Bay in that seventeen-foot canoe. This was what I liked to do. I liked to wander. I was never one to stay in one place very long. Back in 1926, when I was sixteen, I hitchhiked to California. Then I traveled all over the country . . .

Had you read many books about treasure hunting?

The first book I ever read on treasure was not by Rieseberg,* but by Commander Edward Ellsberg, and it was [about] the raising of the S-51 submarine. It's titled, *On the Bottom,* and it's a must if you can get hold of it to read it.† It's very interesting— how they raised the S-51 and lost her and raised her again. And then I read this book by Rieseberg, who has since passed away, you know. His ex-partner was in here the other day.

I suppose at that time you, like everyone else, could only be impressed by what he wrote, because no one knew much about it.

It seemed that no one knew *anything* about it. I had read all about King Tut's treasure, the Aztecs, the Incas, and all that business, and I was always impressed by the story of Cortez and Montezuma, you know. But, I detested history as such.

---

* Lt. H. E. Rieseberg, *I Dive for Treasure,* R.M. McBride & Co. New York 1942.
† New York: Dodd, Mead & Co., 1929.

Anyway, in the summers I was a lifeguard on a big lake in south Jersey. I had gone away to aquatic school and got a Red Cross Water Safety Instructor's training and I was teaching kids to dive. Of course, like most everyone else I built a diving helmet. I took an old can and had a bicycle pump for air and we nearly drowned ourselves. I could do a lot better without that gear. I could swim and free dive with no trouble. I used to live in the water. I used to dive for big freshwater turtles and let them pull me all around the lake bottom, then I'd make them surface. This was the kind of life I lived.

Then one day a big storm came up. It was the aftermath of a Florida hurricane. It struck our area and washed out the dam. As a result two big oyster schooners hit the bridge that connected our city's east and west sides and knocked the bridge out. And of course I came down the rapids in the canoe. Another guy and I shot the rapids during the flood and we hit a piling. The canoe wrapped around it and broke in two. It was a nice cedar canoe, too. We just swam on down the river with the flood.

They brought in a hard-hat diver to survey the damage to the bridge. Since the lake was gone, I was practically out of a job. But I still had to stay on lifeguard duty. The city still paid me to sit up in the tower overlooking all that stinking mud and rotting mussels. My job was to keep people from wading out across the lake and getting stuck in the mud. The newspaper did an article about it. They said I was no longer a lifeguard, I was a mudguard.

Anyway, with the lake gone I was ready for another job. I met the hard-hat diver and told him I was looking for work. He said that I couldn't dive in his gear, but if I got permission from my folks, he would give me a job tending his lines.

That's the way I started, helping him on that bridge job. But I was sure anxious to try out his diving gear. I'll never forget one Sunday when the opportunity presented itself. By then I knew that my boss usually got drunk every weekend and by Monday he wasn't much good. So I washed down his suit Saturday afternoon and hung it up to dry. That next morning I got my friend to come down to the dive barge and give me a hand. I had decided it was as good a time as any for me to go down in that gear. My friend

Art McKee looks over a coral-encrusted dueling sword he recovered on one of his many treasure-hunting expeditions.

helped dress me in the hard-hat rig, started the pump and I went over the side.

It scared me silly. I couldn't see a thing; it was all mud. I couldn't regulate the air when I went down, so I got a pretty good squeeze out of it, still it was a thrill. Finally I decided I'd better come up, but I didn't know how to work the valves. So I started walking up the embankment and got stuck in the mud. I'll never forget it. A whole bunch of guys got together, pulled on my lifeline, and dragged me through the mud. Then we had to scrub down that suit to get it clean. Monday when the diver came to work he said, "Suit's still wet, huh? I don't remember it raining this weekend." And I said, "Well, we must have had a shower."

Anyway, that was the first real piece of diving gear I went down in. Must have been 1934. I worked for the diver for some time on the Delaware River, then I moved to Florida.

What decided you to go to Florida?

I had injured my left knee playing football. They operated on it and took out the cartilage. After that it bothered me a lot. The muscle got small in my thigh and calf, so I went to an osteopath friend of mine. He worked on it three times a week and got the muscles so they would support the joint. He advised me to do lots of swimming to build things up, so I came to Florida where I could swim year round.

I got a job as chief diver on the navy underwater pipeline that runs from Homestead to Key West. Every time it would break down, I would go to work on it. For two years that's where I got a lot of experience in tide diving. Then I became city recreational director in Homestead for over ten years. On my days off I went along the offshore reefs with my hard-hat diving rig and a tug, salvaging old brass and iron off wrecks. One day a commercial fisherman friend of mine, Reggie Roberts, said he had found a pile of ballast and old cannons off Plantation Key. He came up to Homestead and said, "Why don't you come down? I'll take you out fishing and show you a wreck. Bring your diving helmet and see what you can find on it."

Now Reggie knew about this wreck in 1938, and he also knew where there were others. He called them "old cannon wrecks." Well, I got interested in them . . .

Indeed he did. McKee loaded his Miller-Dunn shallow-water diving helmet, hoses, and compressor aboard his tug and headed for Plantation Key. With his friend, they set out for the wreck site. Three and a half miles offshore, Roberts pointed to the long dark shadow of the shipwreck on the ocean bottom. McKee donned his equipment and went over the side. In twenty-seven feet of water he saw what remained of the wreck—a hill of ballast rock about fifteen feet high, forty feet wide, and a hundred feet long. Scattered over the top and protruding from the pile of stones were what looked like old encrusted lengths of water pipe. They were the ship's iron cannon, at least twenty of them of varying lengths. McKee picked around the base of the rock pile, fanning away the sand and pulling out coral-encrusted clumps with odd-shaped pieces of metal and wood fragments sticking out of them. Eagerly he gathered up a bucketful of these items along with several encrusted cannonballs and went back to the surface to examine his finds.

The cannonball was the only thing he could really identify. The rest resembled junk. Still, he loosened a few pieces of the odd-shaped blackened metal from the clumps and thought he would see if someone could tell him what they were.

He took the pieces to a professor at the University of Miami. After close scrutiny the man told him that they were worthless pieces of lead. Not satisfied with this, McKee took the items to a jeweler who promptly identified them as heavily sulphided silver coins.

McKee was elated. On his next dive to the wreck he found a Spanish gold escudo coin as bright as the day it was minted. Stamped on the coin was the date 1721, indicating that the ship had wrecked sometime after that. But what ship?

McKee began searching libraries for whatever information he could find on shipwrecks of that period. Exhausting all the sources he could think of, he started inquiries in Spain. Months passed, then he received a large package from the director of the Archives of the Indies in Seville. It contained copies of old Spanish documents and a photograph of a chart showing not only the wreck McKee had found, but the locations of eighteen others that were wrecked or stranded when the Spanish treasure fleet of 1733 was struck by a hurricane in the Florida Straits.

From translations of the old Spanish documents, McKee learned that the wreck off Plantation Key was the *Capitana el Rui*, flagship of the fleet. His heart skipped a beat when he read that her cargo consisted of over five million pesos worth of treasure. But he was not too happy to learn that all of the treasure was salvaged by the Spanish shortly after the ship sank.

This minor fact did not even slow McKee down. He moved his dive barge over the site, and in his Miller-Dunn helmet he attacked the ballast pile with a vengeance, spending as much as ten hours a day by himself on the bottom undertaking the prodigious task of moving all those smooth river rocks from one side of the wreck to the other, then hand-fanning the sand pockets beside the ship's rotten timbers for treasure and artifacts. Gradually the hard work paid off; his collection of finds grew.

By 1939, with the help of several friends, McKee and his team had moved about 250 tons of ballast rock to get at the artifacts they felt lay beneath the sand. Since hand fanning was slow, McKee tried to think of a practical underwater excavation device that might help them. Recalling that the navy used a device called an airlift to deepen harbors, McKee borrowed the idea and applied it to their needs. Operating on the principle of the vacuum cleaner, compressed air forced into a length of pipe created a suction that dug holes in the bottom far faster than the divers were doing by hand. This was the first time an airlift was used to excavate a shipwreck. After McKee introduced it, every treasure diver used one from then on.

In the following years McKee and his partners recovered an astonishing amount of artifacts and treasure, more of the former than the latter. They had brought up over twenty different-sized iron cannon, more than a thousand silver coins, all dated earlier than 1733, silver statues and religious medals, candlesticks, pewter mugs and plates, jewelry, buttons and buckles, navigation instruments, daggers, swords, pistols, tons of cannonballs and grapeshot, broken crockery, ship's blocks and bits of rope and wreckage, a three-ton anchor, and many more tons of coral-encrusted clusters liable to contain anything from a court sword to a gold coin. McKee had so many items of his shipwreck sacked, packed, or stacked around his premises that he was running out of living space.

I knew I had to capitalize on this thing some way so I decided to start a museum, to make an attraction out of the whole thing. The timbers of that ship were holding the ballast, the cannons and the loot, keeping them from settling deep in the sand, so I began to bring out people in a glass bottom boat to let them watch the divers working on the wreck of a Spanish galleon. That's the way we got our gasoline and provisions.

Then people would say, "Gee, I'd like to go down on that." This was before scuba, see, so I'd say, "All right, I'll put you down." We figured it was worth ten bucks. If the guy paid us ten bucks, we'd put him down on the wreck of a Spanish galleon.

Then we got the idea of not tearing the wreck to pieces. I said, "Let's take the ballast and the cannons, pick them up and put them back on top of the pile to make it more photogenic. Then we started making movies of it. We made a picture for CBS, an hour presentation for the "Odyssey" show; made one for the Hiram Walker people; the Canadian Club thing, "Secret Cargo"; a show for John Craig for "Of Lands and Seas." I went on the "We the People" show and others.

As a result this thing really began to snowball, and I had it all right in the palm of my hand. So I applied to the state of Florida for a lease to protect these wrecks down here because we wanted to excavate them—get the historic relics and artifacts.

Well, by doing this I stuck a knife in myself. We wanted to protect ourselves because we had set up an exhibit, we had the museum here, and we were taking people out where they could watch the operation. It was quite an attraction. There was nothing like it anywhere in the Keys to represent the old history of the state of Florida as reflected in these wreck sites.

We got the lease from the state signed by the governor and the whole cabinet. It said our area extended from the low-water mark to the edge of the Gulf Stream or the ten-fathom line, which gave us the whole area here to operate in and excluded anyone from coming in and tearing up these wrecks. Believe me, I had no love in my heart for history, but I thought, gee whiz, these things should be preserved, the pieces of rope, the sailcloth, the oddities I had got interested in.

We set up our exhibit with the idea of financing expeditions to hunt for more of these historic wreck sites, especially treasure ships. With the lease from the state of Florida, at least we thought we were protected. Then in 1960 I found out differently.

Here's the way it went. Mickey Spillane, a good friend of mine, was down for a few days, and to kill time he was out there helping me clean up the wreck and put back the cannon, getting it ready to film for the Colonel John Craig picture. Craig and I had designed a bangstick together. It was a six-foot-long pole on the end of which was a chamber for a twelve-gauge shotgun shell set

For many years Art McKee said this silver bar came from somewhere east of Key Largo. He found it near a Bahama island. The signs cut into it identify the bar as the anata, *or church tax, from the bishopric of Chiapas, Mexico. Since it was intended for Philip IV, king of Spain, the royal tax of one fifth usually taken by the Royal Treasurer at the Mexico mint has not been removed. McKee believes the bar came from the wreck of a Spanish vessel that had salvaged it earlier from the* Maravilla, *another shipwreck.*

up with a spring. When you hit something with it, boom! Boy, she made a heck of a racket. You had to hold it tight though, or when she went off the stick would go the other way. John said, "I want you to hit a shark with it if you can." That was the idea of the thing: something to keep off the sharks. But since we couldn't find any to test it on we settled for a big moray eel. It blew him right in half.

Anyway, we got the wreck all cleaned up for the film, jetted away some of the sand, brought out two of the cannon I had in the harbor and put them back on the wreck—got it all ready. Then one day a navy photographer and my son joined me for a trip to the wreck on our fifty-four-foot converted shrimper *The Jolly Roger*, which I had rigged with a gin pole, air lift, compressor, the whole thing.

I had heard that Tim Watkins, Olin Frick, and a bunch of his guys we called the River Rats planned to give us some trouble about the wreck. So as we were heading toward the *Capitana*, three and a half miles offshore from here, their vessel, *The Buccaneer*, came out from behind Tavernier Key and headed toward the wreck, too.

The closer we got to it, the more it looked like our two boats were on a collision course. We figured that they were heading for the wreck, too, so we really put on the steam. Later I learned that they had been to the wreck before us, stolen our two cannon and taken my concrete marker with the metal plaque on it that read, "Posted by the state of Florida, our lease number, McKee's Museum of Sunken Treasure, Agent," and according to them, they threw it out into the middle of the Gulf Stream.

When I saw their float I knew it was no crawfish trap float. They beat us to the wreck, but they overshot it. I slowed down, and before they could get back to their float, I had dropped my anchor right where I always did, in the middle of the ballast pile. I was anchored smack over my wreck when they came up.

They went around me like a bunch of Indians around a wagon train, putting up a big wake and shaking their fists. Olin Frick came out on deck carrying a 30-30 rifle. He cocked it and said, "This is loaded and I'll blow your butt out of the water."

In a loud enough voice for them to hear, I said to my son, "Rick, call the Coast Guard."

They came up and anchored right alongside us. I said, "If a diver is down, it is not legal for you to be within five hundred feet of us. I'm asking you to please go off. This is our wreck, and we're going to do a movie on it. If you want to come back and look at it another time, that's all right." I said, "You've been working on the *El Infante* up there, and that's in our lease area, too."

He said, "Your lease, hell. The state has no business giving you a lease and we're going to fight it. We'll see you in court."

I said, "Well, it just might be that way, too." Then I started putting on my diving gear. I told the navy photographer to get some pictures of that guy over there with the rifle. So he took the pictures, and the next day they were in the paper. The *Herald* took one side and the *News* the other and, boy, it went back and forth. A big controversy—a big fight over this wreck.

Finally I went over the side and took that bangstick like I habitually did when I went down. To keep the sand out of the mechanism I tied a Bull Durham tobacco pouch over the end of it. Being a walking diver, I had a lot of weight on to stay down on the bottom.

I looked over the wreck and saw that the cannons and the marker were gone. Then before I could notice anything else, here were five scuba divers coming down on me—the whole crew of the *Buccaneer*! They fanned out, and I was standing there with my back to a mahogany timber we had put on the wreck to dress it up for the movies. It was also a point of reference as a measuring device so we knew where we had worked the wreck. I backed up against that and I looked at them. They had threatened to tear my mask off, but I had on the full-face Scott Air Pac mask with all those spiderweb straps and, boy, it was on snug.

As they started to come in on me, I put my hand up like a traffic cop and they stopped. I didn't want to use that bangstick on any of them, but I patted it. Then I turned around and like a damned fool, instead of getting six feet away, I choked the pole down to three feet and I hit that damn timber and it went *whoom!* Pushed my mask down and bloodied my nose.

I looked around and, hell, there was just one guy left. All I saw was the fins of the others heading back to their boat. I looked back at this guy and he was still there, crouched down like this, see, and I could see a big question mark over his head, you might say, wondering . . .

Maybe he was praying.

Yeah, he was down on his knees, looking at me, see. So I patted this thing. I only had one shot but I started toward him and he took off fast. Boy, if I had a picture of that! He took off and there I was. Boy, I had all the confidence in the world then, see, walking on down that wreck. I had some fifty-five gallon drums filled with artifacts that I had placed back out there with the cannon to recover in front of the camera for Craig's movie. They had tipped them over and taken all that stuff the day before. So I looked all of that over while those guys were up under their boat hanging on the drive shaft and shaking their spearguns at me. And

THE TREASURE HUNTER'S TREASURE HUNTER

all I had to do was pat that bangstick and keep walking around. Of course, the only other shell I had was up in my boat, but they didn't know that. I bluffed them and it worked.

Later, after we came back, I heard one of them say, "Hell, we were scared that you were going to take that other shot and hole the boat."

Well, I said, "I hadn't thought about that, but it wouldn't have done me any good. I'd have had to go get another shell, because I only had that one. It wasn't a double-barrel."

Topside they really cussed me out. Olin got his rifle and blustered around. God, the air was blue out there. Finally my son told me that he couldn't get the Coast Guard. I got the phone and pulled the wire right out of the set to get out the door so that it would look like I was talking and calling the Coast Guard. They pulled out. Bluffed them again, because my radio wasn't working.

When we came in I reported to Craig, who was about to leave for California with his movie crew. I told him how they had torn up the wreck. He said, "Forget it. We'll do it somewhere else. Where do you suggest?" I said Cayman Island would be good. So the Keys lost a good show on that part of it anyway.

Then I called Dan Ferguson's office. He had charge of this thing for the state. They said, "Have them arrested." So I got Charlie Vocelle, a representative of the attorney general's office in Miami. He said he had been told to advise me to see a judge in Miami, to swear out warrants for their arrests and confiscation of their vessel .The state was really gung-ho going to do something.

My lease read "from the low-water mark to the edge of the Gulf Stream or the ten-fathom line." I paid one hundred dollars on that every year. The state got twelve-and-one-half percent of whatever was found. As a result we policed the thing and protected the wrecks the best we could. But everybody was poaching on them. Now, I was all set to take these characters to court when suddenly the state backed down.

Boy, it was embarrassing. I got the warrants all ready. The judge appointed me as an agent for the state to deliver them in Dade County, where they could be served by the Dade County constable. So I went all the way to Miami, found the constable, and they were ready to be served at nine o'clock that night, when Tim Watkins, who owned the *Buccaneer* with Jimmy Green and a little corporation they had, came home.

While we waited, I telephoned my wife and learned that I had had a call from Tallahassee earlier that day. So I called Vocelle at his home and he said, "I hope you haven't served those warrants." I said, "I'll have them served by nine tonight, when Tim comes home." And he said, "I'm sorry, McKee, I've got orders from Tallahassee to withdraw the warrants."

I had spent all that time and money for eight years with the assumption that the state would protect us. But finally it came out that they would protect us not more than three miles offshore. They had been taking our money illegally for eight years because they had no jurisdiction over the wrecks that we were working on over three miles offshore.

And the Capitana *was three and a half miles offshore?*

Right. Of course then they wanted the artifacts and I said, "No, you don't own the ocean bottom out there. You admitted it. You won't protect us more than three miles offshore so we want our money back."

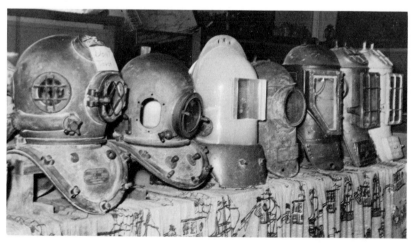

Resembling a medieval knight's headgear, these diving helmets were used by Art McKee during his colorful career. His favorite shallow-water Miller-Dunn helmets are at the far right.

They never would give us our eight hundred dollars back, and in those days it was a pretty good piece of change. To rub it in they threatened to sue our corporation for the remaining two years at one hundred dollars a year. Rather than get into a hassle with them we said, "All right, we'll keep all the relics. We'll pay you the money and let's forget the whole thing."

So that's what happened. After the state said it did not have any jurisdiction more than three miles offshore, from then on we quit working the wrecks out there. We took John Craig and went down into the Caribbean and worked the wrecks on those banks. Then we went down to Jamaica and worked the sunken city of Port Royal.

Was your treasure museum funded from the money gained from the things you found?

Yes. To begin with, the way I happened to pick this place here, we were out taking aerial pictures of the *El Capitana* on a dead flat calm day. I was shooting movies of it with a sixteen-millimeter Bolex out the open door of a Piper Cub when the engine sputtered and the pilot thought we might be about to have some engine trouble. So instead of flying back to Marathon, he flew straight in toward the beach, right in toward the highway, and when he flew over this area I saw this big rock pit nine hundred seventy feet long, two hundred feet wide and eighteen feet deep, as it proved to be, with no outlet to the ocean. I thought, well there is a place to operate from instead of Whale Harbor.

There was no outlet, just solid coral rock, but I bought the twenty-five acres of land, with the pit right in the middle and the whole spread reaching from the highway to the ocean. I got a group of friends together, we pooled our money—no corporation or anything—and dug the channel.

Then we decided we would need more money to operate, so we formed a corporation called McKee's Museum of Sunken Treasure, a Florida corporation authorized to sell twenthy thousand shares of stock at ten dollars a share. A two hundred thousand dollar corporation. I kept fifty-one percent of the stock myself; I now have over eight-one percent.

But the museum was only part of the way that you got treas-

ure hunting to pay for itself. Could you tell what else you did?

Well, after we started taking people out in the glass bottom boat I noticed the tremendous interest, especially when scuba gear came in. I was operating down in Grand Cayman, and people were always on my back, saying, "When can we go with you, McKee? We'll pay five thousand dollars to go, provided we can get a share of what's found."

I thought, here's a good way to get a crew. If I can get a crew together that will put up a substantial amount of money, the psychological effect will be that each one of these guys will be looking to the other to pull his share of the load. No gold-bricking; it's gold hunting, you see. So with each of them paying a thousand dollars, I took eighteen divers on this expedition. We came out of Miami on the boat and went down to Grand Cayman, then on over to the Pedro Bank, where we found a lot of crosses and medallions, but we had bad weather.

Were you working a specific wreck?

Yes. The *Genovés* that wrecked in 1730. She was a vessel out of Cartagena that struck a reef ninety miles south-southeast of Kingston, Jamaica, on Pedro Bank.

We also went there when Ed Link, Barney Crile, and Mendel Peterson worked the sunken city of Port Royal. We were the first ones to work that. Then Link had another expedition. But on the first one I kept my name out of it completely because we didn't want the Jamaican authorities to think that this scientific expedition had a treasure hunter aboard. This was my own feeling. I told Ed that if any newspaper stuff went out I thought it would be to his advantage not to have my name mentioned, because people get greedy and the first thing you know they'd run us off. So we went in there and excavated the sunken city of Port Royal. Link went back later with the barges on the second expedition. But the first one was when we determined that there wasn't any two hundred eighty feet of water and no octopuses down there as the writers had said.

It is interesting to me how you have made treasure hunting work for you in a rather unique way. Sightseers helped finance some of your early recoveries from the Capitana, *which in turn*

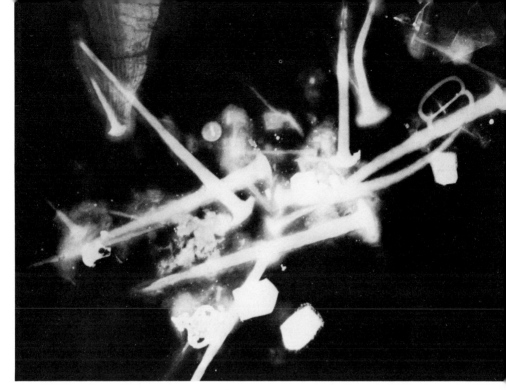

Coral-encrusted conglomerates of shipwreck debris often look nondescript until examined by X-rays, which in this case reveal ship spikes, various buckles, pins, a crown-shaped medallion and the unmistakable angular shapes of Spanish coins. This conglomerate and others have been left as they were found and are on display at Art McKee's treasure museum.

went into your museum to earn more money from tourists. This income plus shared amounts of money from other potential treasure hunters helped finance more treasure hunting expeditions for you, bringing everything back full circle, you might say.

Yes, that's about it. So far I've had thirty-two such expeditions. Right now I'm working up another one.

The silver bars I saw in your treasure vault, did they come from the Capitana, *or one of your expeditions?*

Well now, those three silver bars are quite a story. In the early days, we never told where they came from. We led people to believe that they came from off the Florida coast, but they didn't. They came from over in the Bahamas. Here's the story we figured out after all these years:

Off the Pacific coast near Panama, a ship loaded with silver bars got caught in a hurricane. The ship sank but the silver was salvaged. It was brought ashore, came across the Panama trail to Porto Bello and finally to Cartagena, where it was loaded aboard the *Maravilla*, a ship bound for Spain by way of Havana. When it left Havana, the *Maravilla* came up the edge of the Straits, and near Memory Rock it collided with another ship and went to the bottom, carrying with it the two silver bars I have here in the museum and another one that is now in the Smithsonian Institution, the very same bars that had already been shipwrecked off the coast of Panama.

Once again the silver was recovered, we presume by two small Spanish salvage vessels that salvaged the *Maravilla*. These two ships were wrecked over near Gorda Cay in the Bahamas, where I found the silver bars.

Could you tell me about it?

Well, Charlie Brookfield, who is the past president of the Audubon Society in Miami, came to me one time and said, "How about going to the Bahamas with me and we'll go treasure hunting?" I had my Miller-Dunn helmet, the shallow-water hard hat, see. Charlie said, "I know of a wreck near Gorda Cay where some coins were found which were dated 1651, 1652, and 1653." They were found up on the land and along the beach. He said, "I think there is something over there." He told me he had a colored fellow there who said he had found some cannon. He said he struck the cannon with a rod and there was no rust, that it must be brass.*

So a group of us hired a thirty-six-foot twin-screw Matthews, and we went over there. We hunted around Gorda Cay and found some cannonballs. Then we searched along the shore, talked to Kyle Lightburn [the black] and he showed us the cannon. With the underwater camera we took pictures of them on the bottom. While the others were checking for cannonballs, Charlie told me that he was going off in the small dinghy with Kyle.

A little while later Charlie came back and hauled on my air hose. I came up and he said, "Come on, I think we've found something good."

* Actually bronze.

I got aboard and we went over there in the small boat. Then we moved the thirty-six-foot Matthews over there. I went down in the diving gear and saw a whole pile of ballast. Using a glass-bottom bucket up in the dinghy, Charlie had already spotted an object. He had an eighteen-foot crawfish pole with grains on the end so he stuck it down there in the general direction. I walked along the bottom in the shallow-water hard hat with poor visibility. Taking a mouthful of water I spit it up on the face plate to clear the steam, and all of a sudden I saw what he was pointing at. It looked like a loaf of bread.

I went over and nonchalantly struck it with my hand pick and thought, Gee, that thing's grown to the bottom. I pushed harder and it finally turned over and rolled down into the ballast.

Then I saw the white metal. I squatted down and hoisted up on it. Holy Christmas, it felt like a chunk of lead! I thought, Oh no, this can't be lead. I hit it with the little G.I. pick I had and there it was!

We got a rope on it and hauled it topside. I came right up behind it, and when I got on the ladder I took the bar to keep it from hitting the boat. The bar weighed sixty pounds, by the way; I weighed one hundred and eighty-five at that time, and my helmet weighed seventy-two pounds—all of that on a ladder only meant to support a swimmer.

So the rung broke from under me, but I managed to grab the bottom rung with the bar cradled in my arms before they finally hauled it up. Then I came aboard and they took off my helmet.

By then the guys were hammering at the bar and I heard one of them say, "This has got to be silver!" Then we saw the cross of Spain on it and all the other markings. One of the other fellows said, "Good God, it *is* silver! We're rich!" Boy, we turned around and beat each other on the back, slapped each other around like a bunch of guys that had just won their first football game in high school. Oh, we were excited! One of them said, "Art, is there any more down there?" And I said, "I saw another one," and he asked me what the devil I was doing standing around up there. So I hopped over the side again in my helmet and dropped down to the bottom with my ears banging and crackling from the pressure.

I saw another bar half buried under the ballast. It was under a cannonball sitting there with a big sea fan growing on it. I pulled that aside and there it was. I decided that before taking it out I was going to get a picture of it.

I climbed back up the descending line and had them hand me the Bolex-16 movie camera. Back on the bottom I took the first pictures ever made of the recovery of a bar of silver. Then Mason Armstrong came down in a helmet and took the camera and made pictures of me picking up the bar. That is the bar that was sold to the Smithsonian and is currently on display in their institution in Washington, D.C.

Pretty soon Charlie was overhead in the small boat looking down at us with the glass-bottom bucket. Well, I was cold and I was shivering because I had been down so long, and it was getting late in the afternoon. I was systematically working my way through the ballast looking for more treasure. I went over to one end of the pile, and there was this pole sticking down there again. Charlie Brookfield with his pointer. He was pointing to another bar. So I went over and took hold of the bar. It had a big piece of ballast rock attached to it, and I could hardly move it. The bar later proved to weigh seventy-five pounds, then there was the ballast on it. But I toppled it over, and there on the bar was a small area eaten away by electrolytic action.

I got a look at it in the slanting rays of the late afternoon sun, and, by gum, it was just as yellow as the dial of your watch there. I rubbed it with my thumb and thought, by God, that thing's got to be gold, as heavy as it is. I tied a line around it, and Charlie in the meantime was up there in the dinghy leaning over looking through the glass-bottom bucket and forming words like this: "Are . . . you . . . cold? Are . . . you . . . cold?" Well, I was busy and I had rubbed this thing and saw this yellow because electrolytic action had caused a plating of yellow to go on that silver. By God, I'll tell you what. I'll never find a gold bar without remembering that one, see. Because that eaten away area was just as yellow as any gold I'd ever seen. So I finally picked it up and got it directly under the vessel and helped Charlie by pushing it up. I was looking up and he was saying, "Are you cold?"

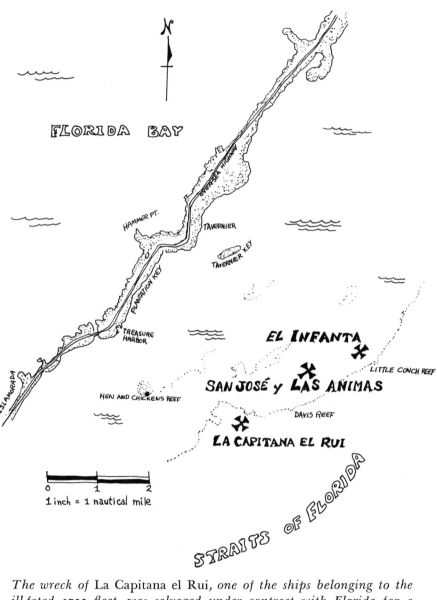

The wreck of La Capitana el Rui, *one of the ships belonging to the ill-fated 1733 fleet, was salvaged under contract with Florida for a while by Art McKee until modern pirates moved in. Note the proximity of two other 1733 wrecks. The* San José, *last to be found, brought on a storm of controversy and trouble for treasure hunter Tom Gurr.*

Finally he got the bar up there and I heard it thump down in the boat, you know, and then Charlie leaned over again and said, "Are you cold?" Hell, I wasn't thinking about cold. I thought, Gee whiz, Charlie said it's *gold*, see. And I can say this: This shows that a guy's never satisfied. I thought, Gee, we found the silver bars, Charlie just said that that one's gold, and if we could just find one made of platinum we would have it made, see? So help me, this is what went through my mind.

Anyway, Charlie immediately took the bar over to the big boat and I was down there furiously hunting. It was getting later and later, the compressor was pumping away, and I was shaking and chopping the ballast away with my G.I. pick when suddenly I brought up the pick and, as I did, I sort of stumbled forward and the pick went right through the face plate. Well, water rushed in, I cut my ear, and finally, of course, I just shucked the helmet and came up topside.

They had to get in the small boat, chase me down tide, and drag me in. I was whipped out, I'm telling you. Boy, that really can beat you. The thing is, when you find the stuff you have no thought about time. It means nothing to you. No feeling. You can cut yourself and you don't even notice it, see. I've seen so many guys that after you find the gold they just get so excited and enthusiastic that you can't reason with them. I had one fellow I'll never forget, in one of my early expeditions—Dick Walker. He was a farmer from some prairie state out west. He always had to have four or five eggs, four or five pancakes, everything, you know. They eat in the morning to last them all day, you know, or all week, the way he ate. Anyway, Dick was a good diver, but he got the idea that he wanted to find some gold. Well down at Pedro Bank you've got a big sea running there, and you get these spikes and nails and when they roll back and forth on the bottom they get really clean and glittery. We had found quite a few of these on our first expedition down there, so I knew what they were. I'll never forget, somebody came up from the bottom and said, "Dick has found a piece of gold." I said, "Well good, I hope he doesn't lose it." I remember worrying about him. Then Dick came topside with it. He said, "Boy, what do you think of this?" He said, "I'm the first one to find gold, right?"

I looked at it and I said, "Walker, I'm sorry, but it isn't gold. It's a bronze-like metal." I said, "I'll tell you what, get me a hack saw." He said, "Oh no, you're not going to cut my piece of gold!" I said, "Now, Dick, don't worry."

One of the other fellows went down and came up with a hacksaw. Walker said, "Wait a minute, let me get a newspaper to catch those gold filings." Well, I started sawing on it and he was catching the filings. I cut it in half and said, "See that. It's one of those pins; there's more of them." He said, "Gee, that's pretty but I still think it's gold." I said, "If the rest of the guys will agree, we'll give you that piece, and you can take it home and have it analyzed." And do you know that the guys wouldn't give it to him. No, they thought it was gold, too! So this is the kind of thing. It's a constant greed, you know. But it's a hell of a lot of fun.

2 ⁓

Kip Wagner: Dragon on the Beach

For many years along the desolate wind-swept Florida east coast south of Cape Canaveral between Sebastian Inlet and the little town of Wabasso, people found odd things on the beach—small, uneven pieces of metal, some so thickly encrusted with a hard black substance that they resembled pieces of broken asphalt. A few finders claimed the water-worn chunks were actually coins, that beneath the black coating the strangely shaped pieces of metal were really silver coins called pieces of eight—Spanish money washed ashore from some long lost treasure fleet. Others, however, scoffed at these claims. One elderly gentleman who customarily walked his dog along the beach said they were nothing but pieces of scrap metal washing ashore from tankers torpedoed along the coast during the war. And he should know—over the years he had skipped some two thousand of them back into the ocean. Spanish treasure? Not likely.

Shortly after World War II, a new arrival to the area was more than a little impressed by the tales of treasure on the beach. He was Kip Wagner, a building contractor from Miamisburg, Ohio, who had come to build a motel in Wabasso. White-haired and wearing glasses, often dressed in white tee-shirts and white trousers, Wagner looked more the part of a retired schoolteacher or ex-navy cook, than a builder. But unlike most visitors to the area, he took enough interest in the local treasure stories to try and track down some of the characters who had really found treasure, such as the man who was said to have found an encrusted bricklike object on the beach and used it in building a fireplace. With the first fire, the newfound "brick" turned to liquid silver. But try as he did, Wagner was unable to find anyone who could actually verify such tales. In fact, it was a long time before he even saw any pieces of the blackened material that people claimed were Spanish coins. And those he finally saw certainly resembled no silver coins he had ever seen before. Yet the stories persisted. What intrigued Wagner was that the blackened pieces supposedly appeared with more frequency on the beach after a severe northeaster scoured the shoreline with pounding surf.

On his days off, Wagner surreptitiously started prowling the beach at low tide, looking for some of the odd-shaped pieces. He looked long and hard, but found none. Then in 1949, an ex-steamer captain, Steadman Parker, told Wagner that he believed he had located the remains of a treasure ship, an old shipwreck near shore, and with Wagner's help, they could salvage whatever treasure might be found on it.

The idea was so enticing that Wagner and three others quit their jobs and immediately got started on the project. The plan was to build a long sand pier out into the ocean at low tide and operate a dragline from there to dredge up the bottom and the wreck.

The partners sank a small fortune into the project and saw it disappear about as quickly as did the sand platforms that were repeatedly washed away, but the group stuck it out until summer's end brought their salvage to a halt. The sum total of their expensive finds amounted to a few wood fragments and a copper maravedi coin dated 1649 that Wagner found on the beach.

Even though his first salvage effort had been a fiasco, the failure did nothing to dampen Wagner's appetite for finding some of that elusive treasure.

The following spring he bought an army surplus metal detector and spent most of his off hours wandering slowly along the edge of the surf, moving the long-handled large metal disk of the detector back and forth, listening for the telltale clicks in his earphones that would announce the presence of a piece of metal on the beach.

By summer's end he had detected a small junkyard of useless metal objects. Then, one day, the instrument signaled the presence of yet another piece of metal, something black, heavy, odd-shaped, the size of a half dollar. Wagner scooped it up and excitedly examined it. How his heart must have pounded, for there, in the palm of his hand, he held the object he had been looking for for so long. A coin of some kind. One side still dimly showed the imprint of a Jerusalem cross beneath its blackened surface. It was a piece of eight! Wagner had found his first treasure on the beach.

In the months that followed, it was a slow, plodding job of beachcombing, but Wagner found at least forty more heavily sulphided silver coins and even a few irregularly shaped gold coins —all of them along the wave-washed sand beach between the little towns of Sebastian and Wabasso, an area Wagner came to call his money beach.

None of the coins were dated later than 1715, but he had no idea where they came from. Were they being tumbled in out of the ocean, or were they actually buried on the beach and washing out of the sand?

To try to shed some light on the mystery, Wagner and a close companion, Dr. Kip Kelso, hired a ditch-digging machine and dug three deep parallel trenches along the beach seventy-five feet long and several feet deep. They found no coins. This seemed to indicate that they were washing in.

Wagner and Kelso scoured local libraries for information. Somewhere they heard that a large fleet of Spanish galleons had

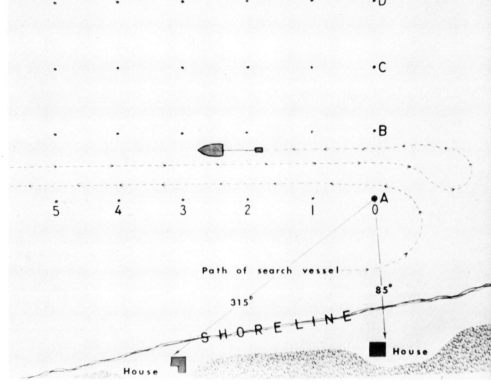

Sketch showing method of "magging" for scattered shipwreck material from the 1715 fleet off Florida's east coast. Grid is established with rows of marker buoys ABCD. The boat tows a supersensitive magnetometer on parallel courses over the grid. Any iron within range of the instrument causes a blip on a recording chart on the boat. These are noted and the areas underwater checked visually by divers. This method is used extensively by all professional treasure hunters. (Courtesy Carl Clausen)

sunk offshore carrying in their holds 14 million pesos in treasure. But when Wagner sent one of the coins to the Smithsonian Institution to see if this story could be verified, he was told that the Spanish treasure fleet that had foundered in 1715 sank in the Florida Keys, not near Cape Canaveral.

Dr. Kelso carried the search further. One summer he went to Washington, D.C., and started going through material in the Library of Congress. From several sources he gradually began to pick up clues. One led to a book written by naturalist Bernard Romans, *A Concise Natural History of East and West Florida,* published in 1775. In the book's flyleaf was a detailed map of the Florida coastline. Just south of Cape Canaveral, Romans had written this notation: "Opposite this River, perished the Admiral, commanding the Plate Fleet of 1715, the rest of the fleet, 14 in number, between this & Ye Bleech Yard." Nearby were the words *el Palmar*, followed by tiny drawings of five palm trees. And in the book, Kelso read this statement by Romans:

Directly opposite the mouth of San Sebastian River, happened the shipwreck of the Spanish Admiral, who was the northermost wreck of fourteen galleons and a hired Dutch ship, all laden with specie and plate, which by [undistinguishable word] of northeast winds, were drove ashore and lost on this coast, between this place and the bleech-yard, in 1715. A hired Frenchman, fortunately escaped, by having steered half a point more east than the others. The people employed in the course of our survey, while walking the strand after strong eastern gales, have repeatedly found pistareens and double pistareens, which kinds of money probably yet remaining in the wrecks. This lagoon stretches parallel to the sea, until the latitude 27:20, where it has an outwatering, or mouth. Directly before this mouth, in three fathom water, lie the remains of the Dutch wreck. The banks of this lagoon are not fruitful.

Kelso was elated. Romans couldn't have spelled it out more clearly. Wagner was equally overjoyed with the news. The stretch of beach Romans referred to could only be that upon which Wagner had found the coins, the strand of sand he called his money beach. The "bleech-yard" was thought to be a place to wash ship's sails.

Seeking more information about the lost fleet, Wagner wrote to the Archives of the Indies in Spain, the largest repository in the world of Spanish colonial records. Though this and other sources, the treasure hunter eventually came into the possession of micro-filmed documents detailing the names and numbers of ships in the ill-fated Spanish treasure fleet, and a detailed account of the treasure manifest, recording all the silver, gold, and precious cargo that the vessels carried. With the help of National Park Service historian Luis Arana, an authority on old Spanish documents, Wagner was soon able to translate the material.

The documents mentioned the presence of an old Spanish salvage site located on the beach opposite one of the main treasure ships. Wagner figured that if he could find that site, perhaps he could then find the wreck just offshore.

He searched diligently for weeks, patrolling the beach high into scrub palmetto so dense that it was difficult for a person to get through. Then, one day, he came upon what was known as the old Higgs site, an area that had been investigated several years before by an amateur historian and later worked archaeologically by Florida historian Dr. Hale Smith. These individuals had indeed turned up evidence of early Spanish habitation, including a buried cannon on the beach. As time passed, other weekend treasure hunters had dug in the area, but so far as anyone knew they had found nothing of significance.

Wagner, however, was not content with simply scratching the surface as others had done. Suspecting that this might be the old Spanish salvage site, he obtained a lease for a half acre of the land, hired a bulldozer to clear away the thick undergrowth, and got busy with shovel and screen doing lots of digging and sifting. Eventually his effort paid off. Among the many pieces of old broken ceramics he found a bullet mold, musket balls, a pair of rusty cutlasses, three blackened rectangular fragments of silver, thirteen silver pieces of eight, and a crudely made gold ring with a $2\frac{1}{2}$ carat diamond setting and six tiny diamonds mounted around the band.

He felt like cheering. Hard work was paying off for him. He knew now from the documents what others had only suspected, that somewhere in the waters right offshore were the shipwrecks he sought.

Wagner built a surfboard with a glass window in it, then swam out into the surf and looked at the bottom. He had hardly started when he spotted an encrusted iron cannon in relatively shallow water. Nearby were four more. But there were no other signs of a wreck.

Leasing a single engine airplane, he had the pilot fly him along the beach while he scanned the shallows for any sign of a wreck. Again he saw nothing.

If it was there, he reasoned, it was buried beneath the sand, probably scattered by the waves and currents. It would take a major salvage effort to recover any treasure, and this involved money, men, and machinery—three things that Wagner lacked. So he filed the information away and made up his mind that within a year he would have the means to start working on the wreck.

To protect his possible find, Wagner made application to the state of Florida for a non-exclusive salvage lease for a fifty-mile area from Sebastian Inlet to a point near Stuart, Florida. The state would receive 25 percent of whatever he found. It was one of the wisest agreements that Wagner ever made.

The winter of 1959 was cold by Florida standards. Many nights in the Sebastian-Wabasso area, divers spent their evenings warming themselves before fireplaces and talking about the treasure hunting they planned to do when the weather changed. Gradually these individuals with a common interest spent more time talking to Kip Wagner. And before the winter was over, they joined forces with him for the express purpose of finding sunken treasure no matter how hard they had to work at it. The nucleus of the small group consisted of part-time treasure hunters Lou Ullian, Delphine Long, Ervin Taylor, Colonel Dan F. Thompson, and Lt. Col. Harry Cannon, the latter two from the installation at Cape Canaveral. While each of these individuals had different vocations, they all had an interest in treasure hunting. Although Wagner had not yet told them everything he knew about his offshore finds, he dived with the group on various treasure hunting trips to other well-known shipwrecks down the coast, and hoped that they were the men he could count on to help him salvage the wreck he suspected lay beneath the sands near Sebastian Inlet.

The men pooled their knowledge and equipment, gradually acquiring the gear they needed for treasure hunting, including a delapidated forty-foot liberty launch, which they patched and painted into a much-needed salvage boat named the *Sampan*.

Soon the divers became proficient in using water jets and moving ballast on old shipwrecks. They found just enough bits and pieces of artifacts to keep them searching for more. Then they struck treasure in a big way, recovering several wedges of silver

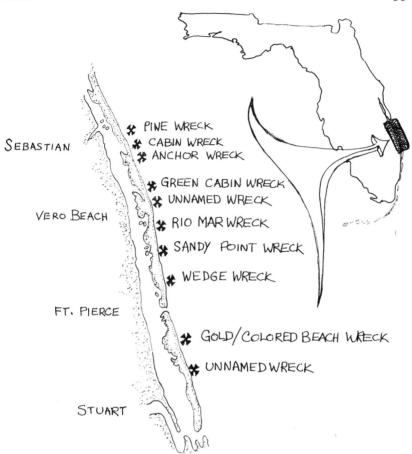

When the 1715 Spanish treasure fleet was wiped out by a hurricane just south of Cape Canaveral (shaded area), the wrecks were scattered along the coast from Sebastian Inlet to just north of Stuart, Florida. Much of the treasure was salvaged by Real Eight and Treasure Salvors, Inc., and what remains is so badly dispersed that it may never be found.

from a well-picked-over wreck near Fort Pierce. Several more followed, so that they had a total of eight silver wedges that fitted together to form a pie, each wedge believed to be worth at that time from $500 to $600 apiece.

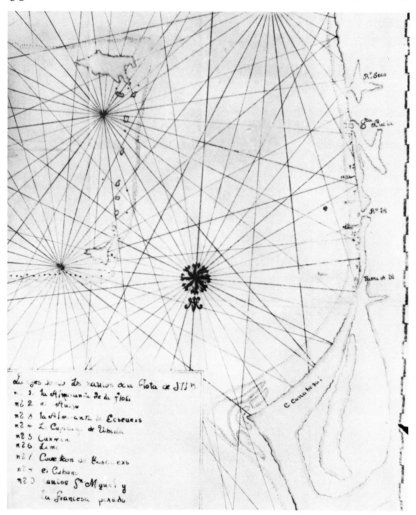

The only known chart showing the location of the 1715 fleet ship-wrecks has all the indications of being authentic and of Spanish origin. In fact it was drawn by archaeologist Carl Clausen after he learned the whereabouts of the wrecks. (Courtesy Carl Clausen)

By now Wagner felt that the divers had become the close-knit team he had been searching for, so he showed them the site he wanted them to work with him near Sebastian Inlet.

As luck would have it, the first time they dived there on a cold day in January 1961, the usually rough seas momentarily calmed and the divers, working in shallow water close to the surf, saw a sight on the bottom that they never expected. Currents and the constant surge of the big winter waves had scraped off several feet of sand overburden and uncovered scattered pieces of the wreck.

Thompson was the first to find a black rocklike object about a foot and a half thick. When he turned it over, he saw a peculiar pattern of parallel lines within the mass. Suddenly it dawned on him that he was looking at the edges of silver coins sulphided together. Other sulphided pieces, apparently coins, lay scattered across the bottom not far from the cannons Wagner had seen earlier from his homemade surfboard. The divers gathered up their finds and hauled them up to the *Sampan*. Thompson's corroded coin cluster weighed seventy-seven pounds and contained an estimated fifteen hundred to two thousand coins. The treasure hunters were beside themselves.

Bad weather over the next few weeks prevented the men returning to the site. When they finally did, the whole thing was covered over again with sand and visibility was about twelve inches. But with their dredging equipment working, they were soon recovering scattered pieces of eight, and Lou Ullian found another clump of coins similar to the one Thompson had found. This one was thought to contain another two thousand silver coins, believed to be worth from $20,000 to $30,000.

After making these valuable finds it became apparent that the weekend treasure hunters were into something more than a hobby. They were deeply involved in the rapidly better paying profession of treasure hunting. Indeed the amateurs now qualified as pros. To protect their interests they formed a corporation named Real Eight, for the Spanish term for a piece of eight, *ocho reales*. Electing officers, the eight charter members made Wagner president.

If not golden, at least the company's future would have a silvery lining, for silver coins predominated over any gold treasure they had hoped to recover from the wreck. But thanks to the whims of Mother Nature, their efforts were not always so fruitful. The next time they returned to the site they found it buried under six feet of sand dumped there by the fickle tides and currents.

That winter the men tried to build more powerful sand-dredging equipment but were unsuccessful. In May, when they returned to the site, they were pleasantly surprised to find that Mother Nature had done the job for them. The sand was gone. Once again the divers had four days to pick goodies off the bottom of the ocean before things changed for the worse and tons of sand covered it all up again.

Searching around for more efficient sand-moving apparatus, one of the divers learned of the injection dredge used by California divers for sniffing out gold nuggets in Western mountain rivers. Using the basic idea but enlarging on it, they developed an air lift in which compressed air was forced up a six-inch diameter nine-foot-long aluminum pipe, creating a powerful suction capable of eating holes into the bottom almost effortlessly. Indeed, the appetite of this mechanical marvel was so prodigious that they named the device the *Hungry Beast*. Through the summer of 1962 they managed to unearth lots of broken pottery, ship's spikes, twenty iron cannon, and several thousand pieces of eight. But when the northers began to blow and the seas became too wild for them to continue their work in the surf, the salvage operation shut down for the winter, and the men returned to their customary weekend activities.

Wagner, however, did not cease his search. He dug out his metal detector and once again started combing the beach for stray coins. On one such cold November morning he was joined by his nephew, Rex Stocker, and the two began their search of Wagner's money beach. For the past few days a strong northeaster had pummelled the Florida east coast and today Wagner felt sure they would find something.

But after a couple hours of looking and not finding much more than bottle caps, Stocker grew restless and started wandering higher above the tide mark, absently kicking at various pieces of jetsam and flotsam carried there by the storm waves.

Suddenly Wagner heard him shout and saw the youth running toward him with something yellow draped over his arm. Wagner first thought he had found a snake, until he saw that it was a long, thin gold chain attached to a peculiar looking pendant. Stocker said he had found it lying in the sand near the dunes.

Excitedly the two hurried home to examine the find more closely. Under a magnifying glass they saw that it was a finely wrought, exquisitely detailed gold chain that measured eleven feet four and a half inches long. Each link was shaped like a tiny flower blossom. The pendant was a three-inch long gold dragon with finely carved scales. Blowing through the dragon's open mouth produced a shrill whistle. Its back swiveled to present a curved toothpick on one end and a tiny ear scoop on the other. Museum experts later appraised the necklace as worth between $40,000 and $60,000. It was the single most valuable find ever to come from the treasure of the 1715 fleet.

To establish a base of operations closer to the site, the group bought a small cabin on the beach, and from then on the wreck they were working just beyond the surf would be known as the Cabin Wreck.

The salvage year 1964 started slowly for the divers, and for the first four months they had to be content to pick up scattered silver coins. But by June the *Hungry Beast* uncovered more clusters of coins. The first conglomerate, weighing seventy pounds, contained about fourteen hundred pieces of eight.. Then a few days after this find, five more valuable clusters appeared that weighed between fifty and seventy-five pounds each. And always as they burrowed into the sand with the airlift, the divers found many fragments of pottery. Wagner had seen similar fragments from the site he had excavated on shore. They were pieces of K'ang Hsi pottery dating from 1662 to 1722. One day, as the men continued excavating into the seemingly endless fragments, they were surprised by the appearance of intact cups, bowls, and saucers of the same kind of blue and white china. Incredibly these pieces had not only survived shipment all the way from the Orient, but they had somehow successfully weathered a hurricane and over two centuries of burial on the bottom of the ocean.

To learn more about the fate of the survivors from the wrecks of the 1715 fleet, state underwater archaeologist Carl J. Clausen (left) supervised the excavation of the survivors' and salvagers' camp on the beach south of Cape Canaveral. He found vital archaeological clues that helped reconstruct the event. (Courtesy Carl Clausen)

Shortly after recovering the intact pieces of K'ang Hsi porcelain, one of the divers noticed a gleam of yellow beside a cannon muzzle. Fanning away the sand he carefully withdrew another gold link chain, this one attached to a small pendant that once contained two miniature oil paintings. Unfortunately, after their long immersion only a faint trace of paint still remained.

This chain and pendant was the first gold found on the wreck. While the divers had turned up thousands of silver coins, Wagner wondered why they had failed to find any gold coins. He did not have long to wait. Thompson and Long, working with the *Hungry Beast* in nine feet of water, soon broke the jinx when their cone-shaped sand hole in the ocean bottom suddenly seemed to sprout gold coins. The divers quickly plucked up twenty-three four- and eight-escudo gold coins. Long topped off the find by picking up a gold ring with an expansion band.

Outside of a couple state officials, no one knew that the men were making these finds. They had kept their secret well. While the locals were aware that Wagner's men were treasure hunting, no one had the slightest suspicion that they were being successful. And the treasure hunters took care to see that the situation remained exactly that way. In the evenings when they came in on the *Sampan,* some of the men kept the curious dockside crowd engaged in conversation while the others quietly transferred the heavy bags of silver coins from their boat to the trunk of their car.

One day early in 1963, a California treasure hunter named Mel Fisher stopped to talk with Kip Wagner. Fisher was returning from a treasure hunt in the Caribbean. He had learned about Real Eight's finds from one of their members, Lou Ullian, who had stopped by Fisher's dive shop in California to discuss excavating equipment used by the West Coast divers. Now Fisher offered Wagner a proposition that both parties felt had merit. Fisher pointed out that Real Eight had more 1715 wrecks in the area that, if found and worked properly, would take more time and effort than Wagner's limited team could afford to give them. Fisher suggested, therefore, that he bring in a group of select divers who would be willing to work a year without any reimbursement, to try and find some of the other wrecks and salvage them, splitting any new finds fifty-fifty with Real Eight.

Wagner liked the idea, and before long Fisher and his crew sold most of their holdings on the West Coast and moved to Florida to start work. Fisher had brought five experienced divers with him: Rupert Gates, Demostines Molinar, Dick Williams, Walt Holzworth, and Fay Field. Each of the men had some specialty besides diving, but one in particular held the key to their fortunes. He was Fay Field, a self-taught electronics expert who had built a proton magnetometer, a device that, when towed behind a boat, detected deviations or anomalies in the earth's magnetic field caused by concentrations of iron such as are usually found on shipwrecks.

Despite the sophisticated electronic device, however, it proved to be a long, unfruitful year for Fisher's group. Finding no treasure to speak of, they became a disheartened crew that saw the

This dragon pendant was the single most valuable item to come from the 1715 wrecks. It is a combination whistle, toothpick and ear spoon, which hung on a complicated floral-patterned gold chain over eleven feet long. The artifact was found just south of Florida's Sebastian Inlet. It was sold for $50,000. (Courtesy Carl Clausen)

Closeup detail of the gold chain attached to the dragon pendant reveals that the 2,176 individual links were shaped as olive blossoms. (Courtesy Carl Clausen)

year they had gambled on gradually drawing to a close. However, a single stroke of luck spared them the ultimate fate of so many unsuccessful treasure hunters.

Two young men not connected with the group, Bruce Ward and Don Neiman, found a perfect eight-escudo gold coin on the beach just south of Fort Pierce. After finding a few more coins, the men immediately took on a companion, Frank Allen, and formed a company, certain that they were going to find a treasure wreck just off shore. But several months of searching revealed nothing.

Realizing that they were operating on a shoestring and that they needed not only more men but better salvage equipment, the three treasure hunters approached Kip Wagner with a proposition. They proposed to show Real Eight the area where the wreck could be found that had produced their gold coins in exchange for a percentage of the finds. Wagner agreed.

Fisher's men were dispatched to the area with the young treasure hunters to see what they could find. A diligent search with the magnetometer turned up nothing. Fisher's crew continued to search for four more months and still found nothing. Finally they told Wagner that they were fed up, that even if something were found their percentage was so small that it would not be worthwhile.

The situation was rehashed with Neiman, Ward, and Allen and a new agreement established in which Fisher's percentage improved while the others agreed to take less.

On this basis Fisher returned to the Fort Pierce site, now armed with a new piece of excavation equipment he had developed called the mailbox. It was a metal box vaguely resembling its namesake which when lowered over the salvage vessel's propeller, directed the prop wash at the bottom in a swirling column of water that effortlessly excavated holes in the sand while hovering divers watched for any treasure that might show up in the craters.

No one really knew where to look. As Fisher often said, it was a big, powerful ocean, and intuition guided their efforts more than anything else. As a result, it was not uncommon for them to find themselves digging areas they had already dug.

One of the 1,300 cedar chests loaded aboard the capitana *of the* flota *of 1715 as it was recovered by Real Eight divers. Each chest contained three bags of gunnysack-type material with 1,000 pesos of four- and eight-real coins in each box. This 250-pound mass of silver coins is firmly fused together from the action of saltwater on the silver. Archaeologists used solvents to separate and clean the coins. The chest was preserved, studied and a reproduction made for museum display.* (Courtesy Carl Clausen)

Then, that April, their efforts turned up the first significant evidence of a shipwreck—they found ballast rock scattered over the bottom a half mile north of where the treasure hunters had suggested they look for the wreck. By the end of the following month they had recovered a hundred silver coins near the ballast rocks, and a few days later, they dug out two solid gold disks, each weighing about seven pounds, with markings from the Mexico City mint on them. Fisher later sold one of the disks for a reported $17,500.

On May 24, Lady Luck came to the divers' assistance in grand

Verification that Kip Wagner had found a wreck of the 1715 Spanish fleet came with this map drawn by Bernard Romans for his book, A Concise Natural History of East and West Florida, *published in 1775. Section shows part of Florida's east coast south of Cape Canaveral with circled note stating: "Opposite this River, perished the Admiral, commanding the Plate Fleet of 1715, the rest of the fleet, 14 in number, between this & Ye Bleech Yard." Arrows indicate present-day Sebastian Inlet and to the south the area of the "Bleech Yard." (Courtesy Carl Clausen)*

These delicate K'ang Hsi Chinese porcelain pieces traveled halfway around the world in the early eighteenth century, went through a hurricane and 250 years on the ocean bottom without the slightest damage. What a tribute to the long-gone porcelain packer! (Courtesy Carl Clausen)

style. As the mailbox blew a crater in the bottom the divers suddenly saw the sand carpeted with gold coins. By the end of the day they had picked up 1,033 of them, and the next day they enriched their collection by 900 more. By week's end they had almost twenty-five hundred gold pieces, the contents of a single chest of gold that had remained where it had apparently been smashed open as the ship's hull disintegrated.

Throughout the remainder of the year, scattered gold coins were turned up by the salvagers but nothing to compare with that first find. One day Mel Fisher dug out what he first thought to be an encrusted ship's timber, but instead the heavy black mass turned out to be a thirty-five-pound silver bar. Then two hurri-

canes brought an end to the salvage season. For the treasure
hunters it had been an auspicious year, to say the least. Their total
finds amounted to thirty-seven hundred gold coins, over two hundred pounds of silver coins, a silver bar, sixteen gold rings, six
silver and six gold ingots, eight pieces of gold chain, parts of two
silver candlesticks, several pieces of silverware, and two silver
plates. In addition, many historical artifacts were recovered. At
season's end, as agreed upon in their contract with Florida, a division took place in which the state received 25 percent and the
treasure hunters, 75 percent of the finds.

Not long after the division, Real Eight and Mel Fisher's
company, now called Treasure Salvors, went to a New Jersey auction with some of their coins and came back to Florida $29,000
richer. After dividing the loot among themselves and paying accumulated bills, the remaining money was reinvested in the operation and the treasure hunters prepared to harvest more coins.

Real Eight reconditioned a new salvage boat, christening it

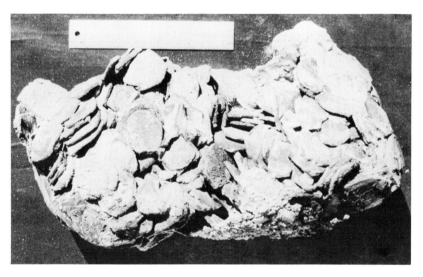

*These two sacks of silver coins from the Cabin Wreck of the 1715
fleet broke out of one of their shipping chests, fell on one another,
and were "frozen" in this shape by saltwater corrosion.* (Courtesy Carl
Clausen)

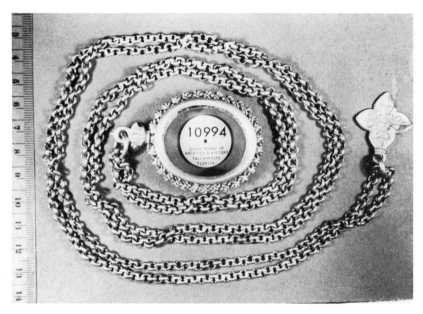

This gold locket, chain, and counter pendant with cross motif was recovered by Treasure Salvor's divers from the Rio Mar 1715 wreck just south of Vero Beach. This is believed to be the probable site of the capitana *of the* Galeones *fleet.*

Opposite top: (A) Pistol, (B) deck cleat, (C) chisel, (D) deck spikes, (E) shears handle. These artifacts, recovered by treasure hunters from the 1715 fleet, have been cleaned and preserved at Florida's archaeological laboratory and are ready for museum display.

Bottom: Silver coins called pieces of eight become heavily sulphided when exposed to salt water. Note how these coins with irregular shapes (due to their being clipped to proper weight) are totally unlike one another and bear little resemblance to contemporary coins. If the sulphiding is not too extensive, treatment with muriatic acid will restore them to nearly their natural appearance. (Courtesy Florida News Bureau)

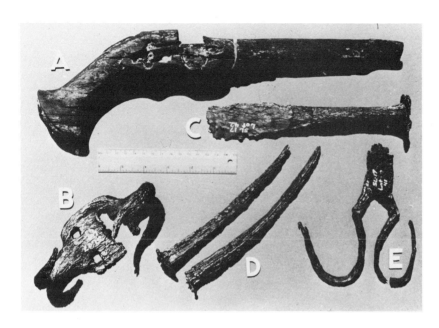

the *Derelict,* and alternated between working the Cabin Wreck and the Fort Pierce site, which they called the Colored Beach Wreck. What made the search extremely difficult in both areas, was the wide distribution of the wreckage over several miles of the ocean bottom. Again no one really had the slightest idea where to look, and intuition was the name of the game. Daily activity continued until a week late in May when they opened up a thirty-foot-wide pit in the bottom with the mailbox and found 130 scattered gold coins in twenty-four feet of water. Moving a short distance away, they tried it again and found an area on the bottom where coins were stacked three and four deep. It was the gold rush all over again. In a single day they recovered 1,228 gold coins, nearly half of them eight-escudo pieces the size of fifty-cent pieces and worth anywhere from $500 to more than $2,000 apiece.

A change in the weather brought a change in their luck. Both were less than perfect. The gold ran out, leaving only scattered silver coins. But a week later the divers were back in the chips again. This time they were all silver. One day, besides silver wedges and clumps of coins, they brought up 665 pounds of silver coins alone. At about fifteen coins to a pound they had almost ten thousand pieces of eight. A few days later this figure climbed to almost a *ton* of silver coins. Still the silver kept coming up.

On July 7 they found the timbers of the old shipwreck plus a 125-pound conglomerate of fused pieces of eight, sixty loose silver coins, two plates, and an apothecary mortar. Then Wagner's nephew, Rex Stocker, made a discovery few people have ever seen and one he himself hardly dared believe. He found a chest of silver.

Once he was sure his eyes were not playing tricks on him, Stocker surfaced and shouted to the others what he had found. Nobody believed him. Everyone knew that teredo worms would make short work of a wooden chest. But when one of the other divers decided to dive down and look for himself, he too surfaced shouting that there was indeed a treasure chest half buried in the bottom.

It was a blackish brown wood packing box less than two feet long, eleven inches wide, and nine inches deep. Part of the top, one side, and an end were missing. But the original contents were still intact—three large clumps of silver coins fused together in exactly the same way they had lain within the chest in bags. The cloth, of course, had deteriorated years ago. The find was carefully brought to the surface, put aboard the salvage boat, and immersed again in salt water until it could reach the state underwater archaeological laboratory at Tallahassee.

Once there, state underwater archaeologist Carl Clausen was able to identify the wood chest as having been made of Central American cedar. From impressions of the cloth bags in the corrosion on the clumps of coins, Clausen made a rubber cast that provided the details for a drawing of the fabric's intricate weave. The coin conglomerates weighed 250 pounds and contained about 3,750 four- and eight-real silver coins.

Salvage work continued until August 1965, when bad weather finally brought the season to an end. The total find that year was more than all the previous years combined. It amounted to 1,958 pounds and 10 ounces of silver coins (more than 37,000 of them), the 250-pound packing case of coins in clumps, 1,782

Kip Wagner examines two silver wedges that weigh from one to five pounds apiece. Near his knee is a "pie" of similar wedges, possibly shaped this way to fit more easily into their wood packing barrels. (Courtesy Carl Clausen)

Aboard Real Eight's salvage vessel, state underwater archaeologist Carl Clausen (second from left) and a treasure hunter pause while spare air tanks are readied for another dive on one of the 1715 wrecks. (Courtesy Carl Clausen)

gold coins, forty-one disks of copper weighing 25 to 75 pounds each, twenty-nine silver wedges, twelve silver cupcakes (ingots so named because of their shape), an assortment of rings, earrings, broaches, and miscellaneous jewelry, pieces of K'ang Hsi china, and thousands of historical artifacts—including ship's hardware, fastenings, and armament. Almost all of the gold had come from the Colored Beach Wreck near Fort Pierce, and all but a small amount of the silver came from the Cabin Wreck south of Sebastian Inlet.

Although other wrecks of the 1715 fleet were to be found by Real Eight and Treasure Salvors in subsequent years, from this point on the returns gradually diminished. With operational expenses running to hundreds of dollars a day, treasure hunting on the 1715 fleet was fast becoming a losing proposition. But while it lasted it did so in grandiose storybook fashion. It was the treasure find of the century, one that gave birth to a whole new generation of eager treasure hunters who unlimbered their face masks and fins and set forth to do likewise.

3 〜〜〜

Mel Fisher: A Carpet of Gold

Incredible as it may seem, Mel Fisher, the most successful treasure hunter in the world, a man who has recovered thousands of dollars worth of treasure a day, is often so broke that once the electric company shut off the electricity in his house because he did not have enough money to pay the electric bill. Another time, lacking funds, he was forced to pay for his groceries with Spanish pieces of eight. Still, Fisher's forte is finding treasure, or at least making the grand search for it. Half his life has been devoted to this endeavor, but it has not made him a rich man. His road to success has been blighted by accidents and tragedies. Yet, in a profession so precarious that few people have ever made a go of it, Fisher tenaciously endures, primarily because long ago he learned the secret of treasure hunting survival. He gambled to find treasure, formed companies, promoted mass stock sales, and poured everything back into the search for more treasure.

With but a slight variation to the theme, it is the same full-circle formula employed in an earlier day by Art McKee, who learned how to eat his cake and have it too. And at this, Fisher is an expert. Rather than stop to enjoy the momentary monetary fruits of his labor, he is always hot on the trail of a bigger and better success. Getting there is not just half the fun for Fisher; it is the whole ball of wax. He gets more pleasure from the quest than from the goal, a not too uncommon trait among treasure hunters.

Born in Hobart, Indiana, in 1922, Fisher grew up and went to high school in Gary, later going on to major in mechanical engineering at Purdue University. When he entered the service at the outbreak of World War II, the army sent him to the University of Alabama to complete his education in the field of engineering. As a specialized army engineer, he served four years in France and Germany. After the war he worked for a while as a government engineer for the Bureau of Reclamation, but it was not a vocation he enjoyed. Yearning to be back in Florida or California where he had learned to dive, he finally went back and picked up where he had left off. And so began his involvement in the field of treasure hunting.

Our interview took place in a backroom booth of Danny's Ice Cream Bar at Key West on a warm March afternoon. Fisher's Treasure Salvors Company headquarters—*The Golden Doubloon*, a 500-ton, 160-foot, three-masted full-size seagoing replica of a Spanish galleon that doubles as a floating museum of sunken treasure—was moored at the wharf just outside.

Fisher, tall, lean, and tan, with gray-brown eyes, a wide, full forehead with receding brown hair, was apparently accustomed to telling the story of his life to reporters, for he seemed perfectly at ease, talking enthusiastically about his early adventures and recent successes. Throughout the entire two-and-a-half hour interview, interrupted twice by long distance telephone calls, Fisher chain-smoked cigarettes.

Tell me how you got started diving.

Well, we were living in Gary, Indiana, and I was about twelve years old when a friend and I decided to build a diving helmet out of a five-gallon paint can turned upside down. I think that was the point where I changed from being a boy to being a man, because I cut the tire off my bicycle, wired it around the can, then melted down all my toy lead soldiers and poured the lead into the tire to get the proper weight to hold the helmet and me under water.

We tried it out in a gravel pit without any faceplate or air hose, and it worked pretty good until I ran out of air. So then I took the valve out of the bicycle tire and bolted it into the top of the paint can. We put on a garden hose and hooked up a bicycle tire pump to the other end. My buddy would sit in an inner tube with the bike pump and pump air down to me while I towed him around the gravel pit by the air hose. This worked okay, even though once in a while my buddy would stick the tire pump under water and I would get a shower.

Then I put a window in the thing. First I just taped it on, figuring that the water pressure would hold it okay. But when I tried it under water the window blew outwards from the air pressure built up inside the helmet. Finally I made a good window for

Mel Fisher is one of the world's most successful treasure hunters, yet he is not a wealthy man. His returns are usually pumped back into the endless search for more treasure.

it, and we had a lot of fun with that rig. Later I built bigger and better helmets and even started a submarine in my basement. Never did finish it. Worked on it about two years and gave up when it got to the complicated part involving CO_2 cartridges and things I needed to stay down very long.

Let's move ahead a bit and pick up on your activities when you left your job with the Bureau of Reclamation.

Well, being in Denver, Colorado, at the time, I mainly disliked being away from the water. I couldn't stand it. There was no place to swim or dive. So I moved to Tampa, Florida, and became a building contractor on various small construction jobs there. I lived in Tampa for four years, and that's where I really got interested in diving and spearfishing.

After a while I decided just to quit working altogether, sort of like the hippies do today. I took about a six-month vacation to do nothing but beach-bumming, diving, and spearfishing. I really enjoyed it. No responsibilities, nothing to do but just go off and dive. That's when I acquired my first Aqua-Lung. When they first came over here, I got the sixth one that came into the country. I drove from Florida to California to buy it.

Finally my folks and I moved to Torrance, California. My dad wanted to build a chicken ranch. He always wanted to try chicken farming. So I helped him build it, and we got in about five thousand laying hens and four thousand fryers and went into business. I hadn't used my GI Bill and education so I took a night school course in poultry husbandry and agriculture and ended up getting a degree in that field.

We were in that business about four years, but I still kept up with the diving as a hobby. I built a machine shop in one of the feed sheds and did some research, designing and development of powerheads, CO_2 guns, and rubber-powered Arbalete-type guns for spearing fish. I got a punch press, a drill press, along with other machinery, and started manufacturing this type of diving equipment for jobbers and distributors in the Los Angeles area. It reached the point where I was making more money in working a couple hours with my diving-equipment business than I was in working the remaining twenty-two hours with the chickens. So I opened up a retail store in another feed shop, the first specialized skin diving shop in the world. I started teaching people how to dive and selling them equipment and filling tanks.

Business was booming, so I built a store in Redondo Beach, California. It was really a good business, I had the only dive shop in California. People would be waiting in line when I got to the shop in the morning. We worked to midnight every night teaching people, thousands of people, how to use scuba gear. Of course, the main idea was to sell them all diving equipment. I got interested in underwater photography and did a lot of that as a hobby, then pretty soon they began asking me to show these films on TV, which I did. And as it happened, for four and a half years I had my own television show, showing these movies I'd made. Some of them were about different expeditions that I went on. I'd take a group of people up in the mountains to dive in the rivers for gold and make a movie about it.

I invented a very good gold-dredging machine and made a lot of money with that, then made and sold these gold-dredging units for divers. I made a movie about diving for jade at Jade Cove in California; another about going down to La Paz and spearing big giant sea bass. Made another show about going to Acapulco diving, and that's one of the first spots where I got interested in treasure hunting. I was just sitting on the beach relaxing, and a little Mexican boy came up and told me about a Spanish galleon out there in Acapulco harbor. I was kind of bored, just sitting there watching those bikinis go by and . . . you know how that is, once you've seen one you've seen one.

So I decided treasure hunting would be more fun. I went out and didn't find anything, of course, but I really enjoyed looking. I enjoyed the hunt. I guess I still do, because I'm still on the hunt all the time. Similar to some of these guys that go hunting for polar bears or elk, except that I'm hunting for old Spanish treasures. I enjoy the history of it and the archaeology aspects. I'm not an archaeologist by degree, but probably should have been because that's the field that fascinates me the most.

Did you have any luck finding anything at Acapulco?

No, we didn't. We found a couple modern ships. First we

thought they were Spanish galleons, but as it turned out they weren't. This got me interested in the archives in Acapulco. You see, that's where the galleons used to come in that made the trip over to the Philippines once a year . . . took them three months to get over there. They would load up with five or six hundred tons of valuable items, and then it would take them nine months to get back across the Pacific to Acapulco, the first good sheltered harbor that was close to the Mexico mint. Some galleons were sunk there, but I never went back to search for them because the Mexican government is very jealous of their history and artifacts and they won't let anybody take anything out of the country. So I've never gone back there because of the restrictions they have. They take one hundred percent of what you find.

That's a pretty nice chunk.

Yeah, there's still literally hundreds of galleons and other wrecks along the Mexican coast, but they still will not allow anyone to take anything. Maybe someday they will get at it themselves. Meanwhile all that history is just laying down there.

After your trip to Acapulco, did you come back then?

Yes, I'd just go from two weeks to a month on each expedition. Made a three-month trip to the Panama area, and this was a rather serious treasure hunt. I had my own sixty-five-foot yacht that I bought for the purpose.

Was this your first initial big hunt after your Acapulco experiences, or were there others?

No, I had made several other trips also.

But you started getting interested from that point on?

Yes. I guess the next one was a search on a reef out of San Diego—Cortez Banks, about one hundred twenty miles out at sea where the reefs come up near the surface. One of those Manila galleons is supposed to be there. I was rather new in the business then, although I did have a magnetometer. I found out that that reef was very magnetic, and I couldn't use the mag successfully because of that. So we made a visual search and found other modern wreckage, but no galleons.

When did you acquire the mag?

Well, I had inquired of all the detector companies in the

country, and none of them had anything that would find anything at any distance, so one of the guys . . . well, I worked with them on research and development and I tested things for them . . . I'm trying to think of the name of the outfit . . .

Was one of the military mags the first one you got?

Yes, it was. I got one called an ASQ-1 used to find submarines. I went out to Arizona, where they had a whole flock of surplus airplanes that they were scrapping. An outfit bought the planes, melted down the aluminum and reclaimed it. They had tons of equipment. I searched through it and picked out a whole pile of stuff I hoped would make up the magnetometer, gave them a thousand dollars, and took a whole truckload back to California.

Then I found a guy that understood electronics and got him to rig one up for me. His name was Lou Black. He's quite a sharp guy. Then a little later on I got an ASQ-3 which was a little more modern, then an ASQ-5 and an ASQ-12. I believe they are still using the last one in the military today for locating submarines, but they also have newer types. It's very complicated equipment, very hard to maintain. They are large and cumbersome. It takes a very talented man to keep them running.

In California in my store I started a club of guys that either wanted to treasure hunt or salvage. Each week I'd take out a different crew. We had one hundred twelve men in the club. We'd practice with all our detection and salvage gear. I had kind of a rotating crew that would take off a day from work about once a month. We'd schedule it so I had a crew every week. All the materials that we salvaged we sold and split the profits.

What kind of things were you salvaging? contemporary things, brass, et cetera?

Yes, we salvaged some huge bronze propellers and monel shafts. One day we found a big wreck out in the channel at about a hundred feet deep, and it must have had two thousand modern fishing anchors on it from guys who had anchored there to go fishing. So we brought up about two thousand anchors in one day.

Another time we went out and located one of Al Capone's gambling ships that he had anchored three miles off of Long

Originated by Mel Fisher, these units mounted on the stern of salvage vessels revolutionized treasure hunting underwater. Variously called mailboxes, blasters, blowers or dusters, in use they swing down so that screened ends of the elbow pipes fit over the vessel's propellers. With the vessel firmly anchored in all directions the prop wash is then funneled toward the bottom in a swirling tornado of water that rapidly excavates holes in the ocean floor.

Beach, California. He had shuttle boats going back and forth hauling people out there to gamble. His rival, another gangster, had a boat anchored off of Santa Monica. It was called the *Star of Scotland*. One night this gang from the *Star of Scotland* went out to Capone's ship and blew it up.

About a week later, Capone went out and blew up the *Star of Scotland*. They had a kind of gang war going on. I went back through the archives in the newspapers and got all the news stories about it. It was interesting. Before she was sunk, the governor of California took a crew out and tried to raid the *Star of Scotland*, but the guys on the *Scotland* turned fire hoses on them and threw cargo nets over their boats. They never did stop them. It took another gang to do it.

We went down on Capone's ship and found roulette wheels, Chuck-a-Luck machines, cash register, all kinds of stuff we brought up. I've still got part of the roulette wheel in the museum here.

Was it a large ship?

Pretty large. A couple hundred feet. It was kind of spooky going down through the hatches and inside where it was pitch black.

What depth was it?

About sixty feet. We found money in the cash register. I took that out and set the machine in front of the store and somebody walked off with it. It was a real antique.

We found all kinds of things out there with those detectors. It's amazing how much stuff is in the ocean. But that was just practice, more or less to get all our equipment working, to get the experience. Then we would go on expeditions once or twice a year in earnest to try and find treasure somewhere or other . . . as I mentioned about Panama. That was a three-month expedition and I wasn't too familiar with what expeditions cost at that time. I had a twenty-four thousand dollar budget for the trip and it cost fifty-four thousand dollars, so I went in the hole. It took me two years of hard work to pay off all the bills and debts I had on that expedition.

I made three different expeditions to Silver Shoals. That reef is about three hundred miles north of San Juan, Puerto Rico, and about a hundred miles east of Porto Plata, Dominican Republic. On the charts it says, "Dangerous reefs. Stay away from this place." It is very treacherous.

Were they old or modern charts?

Modern charts. I have the old charts, too. That's where Sir William Phips found treasure.

Did you have any documentation when you went down there?

Yes, I had all of Phip's records and several other books and things pertaining to it. I'll tell you how I picked that spot; it was kind of peculiar. Me, a friend of mine, and our wives were lying on the floor in our living room one night and we said, "Let's go on a vacation together." I said, "Why don't we make it a treasure hunt? It'll be more fun." They said, "Great! Where are we going to go?" Well, I had a huge atlas about treasure hunting and treasure maps and I said, "I'll just close my eyes, open the atlas and point and we'll go there." So that was the system. Very scientific. I opened the atlas and pointed my finger and it was Silver Shoals.

We read what the author wrote about it. He said, "There are twenty-one galleons with two hundred million on them," and I said, "Well, that's good enough." I had no idea what it took to stay for three months out at sea with no spare parts, the food problem, and so on.

That was the first of several trips there?

Yes. I made three different trips. The first trip we never quite got there. There were four couples of us. We drove across from L.A. to Miami, chartered a sixty-five-foot boat, the *Kilroy*, and went out to Nassau, which was a trip in its own. Then we went on down through the Bahamas to Great Inagua, where we took on fuel by dugout canoe. We continued down to Port de Paix, Haiti, refueled and got supplies, then went to Ile de la Tortue, where the pirates had a stronghold for about two hundred years. No government dared send their forces in there because it was completely run by pirates. They had their own fort and harbor and everything.

We got interested in using the metal detectors around the fort and in the caves where the pirates supposedly stashed a lot of treasure. Diving near the island we found six wrecks with cannon, so we dug on those. Our captain refused to go out to Silver Shoals because he was afraid to . . . wisely, so, probably, because at that time we weren't too familiar with what it took to be out in a place like that. Anyway, before we came back to Miami we found a few things, cannonballs, cannon, swords—things like that. No gold.

Then we had another trip there with a captain who owned the boat works in San Pedro, California. This was pretty well organized. This time I had Fay Field, Rupert Gates, Demostines Molinar, Dick Williams, Walt Holzworth, and a lot of good men with me. We went out there for sixty days and did pretty good. We found some wrecks and did a little digging, got a few nice artifacts.

How big is the reef?

It's a huge area. Silver Shoals is seventy miles long, fifty miles wide, and there are millions of niggerheads that come up just under the surface . . . very treacherous. The plateau itself is sixty feet deep, but all those niggerheads come up to where it is about waist deep. Naturally that's what catches all the ships. It's a beautiful, fantastic reef . . . all kinds of tunnels and beautiful live coral. But most of the wrecks are covered with from ten to twenty feet of live coral, completely encrusted over. So it is very difficult to get at them. That was one major problem.

Had you found any coins yet at all?

We found a few coins but nothing fantastic. We always found a few coins. It turned out that this wreck was the same one that was visited just a few years ago by Jacques Cousteau. I had invited Cousteau to go with me on that expedition, and he said he would dearly love to but his life was written on pieces of paper. He had signed so many contracts that he was booked up for the rest of his life, so he couldn't go. But evidently he switched around the contracts three or four years later and got one so he could go treasure hunting at Silver Shoals.

Of all the area out there and the hundreds of shipwrecks, he found the same one that I had been working on. He was digging a hole there and he found a weight belt that said Mel's Aqua Shop, which was my store in California. He called me up when he got back and asked me if I'd ever worked this wreck and I told him yes. He said he didn't have enough footage for his TV show and wanted to know if I had some extra film. I said I did, so we got together on that.

Anyway, we still didn't find any pile of gold or anything. Just a lot of nice artifacts. But it was a lot of fun.

You might mention what Fay Field was doing about that time.

Fay came into my dive shop one day talking about finding shipwrecks and asked me about my magnetometer. He said he wanted to find some sea shells for his wife, a kind that lived in shipwrecks.

The spiny oyster?

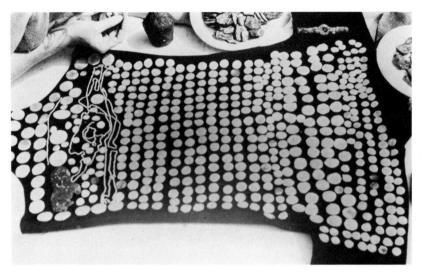

Not holes in the jacket of a diver's wetsuit but gold coins neatly lined up along with several sections of gold chain, a king's ransom dived up in one morning on the 1715 gold wreck found by Treasure Salvors south of Fort Pierce. Other items include two dishes of sulphided silver coins and a silver "cupcake" so named because of its molded shape. (Courtesy Carl Clausen)

Yes, they are beautiful sea shells. So I invited him to come out with us. He got interested and said, "I think I'm going to build a magnetometer that's not so bulky. It might work a little better."

He had some electronics background?

Yes. He didn't have a degree, but he had good common sense. He knew about electronics, so I told him I'd furnish all the materials and pay for everything if he would build it and we'd go fifty-fifty on it. He said, "Fine." So he built it and I paid for it and darn if the thing didn't work. It was a lot handier, smaller, and more portable. It worked a little better than the ASQ-12 that I was using at the time.

Fay's detector gave us something even better than what the military had. Eventually we got patents on it, and not so long ago we sold the manufacturing rights. At this point it is highly sophisticated, the ultimate in detection or search equipment for use in the ocean. We tested it at the navy and army labs and at Union Carbide. According to all these lab reports, we've got the best there is.

We've done an awful lot of research and development on gold and silver detectors. As of this date we do not have a proven detector that will find gold and silver at a long range, although we can find iron at a quarter of a mile easily. But I believe we have one now, in the lab, that will reach out a quarter of a mile and find silver or gold.

We're setting out a buoy pattern today on the *Atocha* site. We plan to take out this new detector and try it very shortly. If this instrument succeeds it will be a new breakthrough in the industry. We should be bringing in billions and billions and billions of dollars worth of gold and silver because it's all out there. It's been estimated that one third of all the gold that has ever been mined in the world has gone down in the sea. And that's a hell of a lot of gold.

My historian, Dr. Gene Lyon, is so far ahead of me on the research for our corporation that he's got about fifty sites for me to work in. I plan to research about fifteen of these sites this year and make a feature movie of it for the theaters.

Let's jump back to Silver Shoals again—the trip out there with the group. You found artifacts but nothing of treasure value, right?

Yeah, that's right.

You came back to the states. Now did you make another trip out there?

Yes, we made a third trip for ninety days.

Were you more or less just going there and searching the general area for wreck sites, or was there some specific part of the reef that you were going to or were interested in?

Well, both. The third time we started working, we continued on where we left off on the previous expedition. Also, I would take off with my wife, and we'd go down the other end of the reef and all around with a magnetometer and a small boat. We would locate new sites and check them out.

There are a lot of wrecks out there, and it's very difficult to determine whether they are ancient or modern because there is so much live coral over everything. There are also a lot of sharks.

I've been with sharks all my life. They used to call me Fearless Fisher because I'd wrap my legs around them and stab them and kill them. I'd chase them away and hit them over the head with a sledge hammer and fight them with an axe and all kinds of ridiculous things for the movies when I went on these filming or treasure hunting expeditions, which I did every year. I always took underwater movies. When I brought them back to California, I could sell any footage with sharks in it for ten dollars a foot, and any footage with a shark and a man in it for twenty dollars a foot. This paid for my vacation more or less, and I had no fear of sharks. They all seemed to be afraid of me. But at Silver Shoals I changed my mind . . . there were so many of them.

Thanks to the Shoals we lost all of our anchors, ground tackle, chains, and heavy lines. I thought I remembered where we lost one of our anchors, so we went searching for it with a mag and found it. There was Demostines Molinar, George Gilette, and myself on a small boat.

These crazy sharks started circling around us when we anchored, about three or four dozen fins circling around the boat we were in. I told the guys, "Well, I'm not afraid of sharks, but it just doesn't look prudent to go in. There are so many of them circling around us. I've never seen that before."

Mo was the same as me. He said, "I'm not afraid of sharks either." (He came to my aid several times with sharks.)

He jumped in and went down and all the sharks followed him. His bubbles were coming up fine, and it looked like he was all right. Then George jumped in and there I was, on the skiff by myself. I thought, "Well, I guess old Fearless Fisher has to go in, too." I jumped in, sank down, and immediately a couple dozen of them came up to look at me.

I backed up against the coral ledge and sank deeper. When we got down deep, they didn't seem to come close to us, but they did keep darting in.

George Gilette had an underwater still camera. He went down deep about seventy feet and was taking pictures of us.

Mo and I went to the anchor and I tied a lifting bag onto it. I had an extra Aqua-Lung tank that I filled the bag with. Meanwhile Mo was pricking off the sharks with a shark pricker, which is a hand spear that doesn't have any prongs or barbs on the end of it. Instead it just has an inch of point and a flat washer welded onto it so it can't go into a shark. As they would come in close enough, he would hit them on the nose and they would take off. Usually if you hit one on the nose you wouldn't see him any more. He pricked three or four of them while I was trying to get the anchor up.

One of the anchor's flukes hooked on a ledge of coral. I couldn't get it loose because the lift bag was holding it up. Mo set down the shark pricker to help me shake the anchor loose, and all of a sudden the ledge broke and we went up together.

Mo went back down to get the pricker. When I got to the surface, about two hundred sharks of all sizes and several different brands started coming at me. I got scared and headed for the boat, which was only about thirty or forty feet away. The sharks reminded me of puppy dogs, they would come at me, and I'd hit them on the nose with this spare tank I had and they would turn around and run. When I started to swim they would come again. I would turn and go at them and they would turn around. It was back and forth.

Two of the sharks came up behind me, nudged my arm, and went to take a bite. I jerked it away like, "No, you can't have that!" Another one came up behind me and nudged at my leg. I jerked it up and he missed.

I got to the boat and went to jump aboard, but I had about fifty pounds of lead on so I could stay down and work. The end of my belt had gone through a loop, and when I jerked it to take my belt off it tied into a knot.

Three or four of the sharks came up and nudged me all at once. They all tried to bite, so I jumped for all I was worth. I got up with my rear end on the edge of the skiff, but my legs were still in the water. The sharks tried to grab them, so I lifted them up and fell back into the water.

My stomach knotted up, I was so scared. I just thought to

Recovered by Treasure Salvors from the Colored Beach wreck of a ship belonging to the 1715 fleet, these gold escudos show the crude manner in which the coins were struck, many failing even to show the date of their minting. (Courtesy Carl Clausen) Right: The reverses of the same set of gold escudos show the Jerusalem cross and marks where the coins were trimmed with shears to their proper weight. Unlike silver coins, the gold pieces glimmered as bright as the day they were minted. (Courtesy Carl Clausen)

myself, "I'm dead." I was completely exhausted and scared to death.

I sank down in the water and let all my air out. I was weighted heavy and that made me go down pretty fast.

When the bubbles cleared, there was Mo pricking sharks like mad. He was just pricking sharks everywhere. There must have been a hundred or two hundred of them. I thought, "Good old Mo, that's about the fifth time he's saved me."

He untangled my weight belt and I got my gear into the boat. Then I took the shark pricker and pricked them off while he got his gear off and we got in the boat.

George Gilette, the photographer, surfaced. He had been taking pictures of all this. He was down on the bottom shooting up and they didn't bother him. He came up and hung his arms on the edge of the boat, and I said, "George, get out of there. Didn't you see those things?" He said, "Yes, but I'm not afraid of sharks."

I told him the anchor was stuck and he volunteered to go get it. I said no, but he went down anyway. He unhooked the anchor and came back up, and here came the sharks crowding him. Mo and I grabbed him and heaved him out of the water, tank and all, and flopped him on his stomach in the boat. He said, "I've changed my mind, I'm afraid of sharks." I said, "Me too."

Those Silver Shoal sharks really discouraged us. About six of them would move in on the wreck every morning and be there when we got up. We threw in a stick of dynamite just to scare them, but it just killed a few little fish and more sharks came in. We threw ten sticks into these sharks to kill them all. But it brought in about a hundred more sharks. In a little while it was just a solid mass of sharks. That knocked us out of about three days work on the galleon out there.

Finally we found a system that worked pretty good. We would only put out an electric dynamite cap and explode it. This was enough to freak them out and make them leave; it didn't hurt anything or kill any little fish. So we got back to work.

On the third expedition we chartered a huge sailboat over one hundred feet long and an old boat similar to a shrimp boat. We went out there and worked for three months and still did not come up with any far-out treasure. We also made expeditions to Yucatan, made movies of diving in the sacrificial wells and cenotes. We went to different Mayan ruins.

Did you find anything in the cenotes?

When we arrived at Djebilchaltun, Dr. Morgan was there with Dr. Andrews. Andrews had cut some trenches and was dusting off a skeleton. A lot of Mayan Indians were taking things, and they did not want Andrews or us to have anything. It had to do with their religion, I suppose. When we brought things up out of the well and set them there they would disappear. We'd go down and come up with something else and that would disappear.

Was that before Marden and Littlehales got down there to do their story for National Geographic?

Yes, about a year before that.

We also had a trip to a place called Lake Petén Itzá, Guatemala. I intend to go back there again this year. A lot of fascinating history of the Mayan civilization is there. I have a feeling we may unlock a few thousand years of it, because that was one of the last outposts of the Mayan civilization. The Spaniards could not get at them on that island. I dived there from a dugout canoe and found some old things. Thousands of items were thrown into the lake to keep the Spanish from getting them. Then when the Spanish came in, they completely annihilated all the Mayans on the island and threw everything else that was left into the lake. They were under orders from the king of Spain to destroy all history records and all idols and things of their religion. And the Spanish did a pretty good job. Almost all of the Mayan records were destroyed. I think only three books, the codices, are left now, and they are not decipherable. So we may pull out some real good history from that lake.

I also want to work a place called Saint Eustatius, south of the Virgin Islands where there is a sunken city similar to Port Royal and from about the same period. It was a health resort in those days, with hot baths where the wealthy people went to cure their arthritis. They had a gambling casino and some wealthy stores and it all went under. So we'll probably do something there.

You were coming back from a trip to Silver Shoals when you stopped to see Kip Wagner, weren't you?

That's right. Yes.

Let's get into that phase a little. What year was that?

Well, I went to see Kip every year. As I went through Florida, I would stop and talk with him.

Had Lou Ullian come by your shop in California?

Called "Royals" by treasure hunters who believe these finely struck gold coins may have been intended for Spanish royalty, these perfectly made pieces were scarce enough among the 1715 treasure find to make them worth several thousand dollars apiece. (Scale in inches.) (Courtesy Carl Clausen) Right: The letters just to the left of the royal crest on this finely made gold eight-escudo "Royal" indicate that it was minted in Mexico. Dated 1702 and bearing the name of Philip V, king of Spain, the coin was recovered from the Colored Beach wreck of the 1715 fleet. (Courtesy Carl Clausen)

Yes. Lou came by my shop out there and he knew that I had invented these vacuum dredges that were working pretty good.

Was that the injection dredge?

Right. He wanted some advice on what to do, so I stopped and asked Kip what the problem was. He took me out to the Cabin Wreck near Sebastian Inlet and showed me the depth of the water and the rise of the land and the fall on the other side. So I designed a dredge system that could be operated on land to vacuum off the wreck and run everything over sluice boxes.

Kip asked me if I would come there and work. He explained to his group, who all had full time jobs and only got a chance to go out on Sundays, that he needed somebody in there full time. So I brought this hand-picked crew down. From the one hundred

twelve members I had in my club I picked the six best men. We
sold all our assets and moved from California to Florida. I sold my
business, my yacht, my home, my extra car, and everything I had—
paid off my mortgages and time payments and just cashed out.
The other guys did the same. We just came to Florida and said,
"Kip, here we are. We're ready to go."

He was kind of surprised that we actually did that. We made
a pact between us that our group would chip in on expenses and
would work for one year with no pay and see what we could do.
Before this, our longest expedition was ninety days, so we figured
if we had a year, we could succeed.

But after three hundred and sixty days went by, we ran out of
money and started going into hock. Five days before our time was
up we tried out this mailbox dusting machine that I had invented.
We turned it on for fifteen minutes, then went down and the
ocean was paved with gold . . . there was gold everywhere.

That was a big day. We developed this machine basically to
take clear water down to the bottom because the water was very
murky. When we used our other dredges that I had developed,
you couldn't see what you were doing, you had to feel everything
to see if you could find a coin.

So the first time we tried that thing out we were on a wreck in
fifty feet of water. The top layer of water, the first ten feet, was
crystal clear, but the bottom forty feet was very muddy. We knew
that there was a wreck down there, but we didn't know what it
was. So we turned this machine on, and as the prop wash went
through the elbow and down, it drove a column of clear water
down to the wreck. We drifted down the column and, much to our
amazement, as we sat there this bubble of clear water got larger
and larger and pretty soon we could see the whole wreck from one
end to the other and everything on it, all the fish and everything,
when before we couldn't see a thing.

Then we took it in to where we had found one piece of eight
on the galleon and turned it on there. And that's when we found
the big bonanza.

What wreck was it that got clear as you used the duster?
That was a wreck off Fort Pierce Inlet.

The Wedge Wreck?

No, it was not a galleon type. It was a modern barge loaded with tools and other equipment.

You were just trying it out then?

Yes, that's right.

So when we really hit it big, the bottom was paved with gold. Everybody jumped overboard.

How did you get on to that particular site?

Well, we were working the Sandy Point Wreck and had found some treasure there. I found one gold coin at Sandy Point, and that's the one I have mounted on my ring here. A one-escudo coin. I was real proud of that, because after a full ten years of treasure hunting without finding a gold coin I had finally found one myself, so I bought it from the company and had it mounted on that ring. That's the seed that grew into the money pile.

The next day Walt Holzworth found a one-escudo coin. Then we found a pocket with a whole chestful of pieces of eight, but they were badly worn. We found a bronze bell from the galleon and a few cannon. We dug around there for another couple of months and didn't find anything else. It was very disappointing, that after thinking we were going to find treasure, we didn't.

This was at Sandy Point?

Yes. Kip Wagner came on board and said that he had just signed a contract with four fellows that were beachcombers that had found some gold coins on the beach south of Fort Pierce. The contract, I believe, was fifty-fifty. The beachcombers would get half and Kip would get half. At the time, that area wasn't included in Kip's search contract with the state. He had a non-exclusive search area from Sebastian Inlet to Fort Pierce Inlet. This was south of there, but he said, "I'll go ahead and check it out."

So one of these guys came out with us on our boat and we went down there. He saw debris in the water and said, "The wreck's right down here." We went down and there wasn't any wreck there. So then we just gave up on it. We told them that according to the present arrangement, if we found anything and they took half, the state took a quarter, and Kip took half, there wasn't anything left for us. And we were paying all the bills and

Small gold bee with emerald was found by a beachcomber near the 1715 Colored Beach wreck. The emerald is thought to be Columbian because of the characteristic flaw discernible in the gem. (Courtesy Carl Clausen)

doing all the work. So they signed a new contract where they would get, I think, five percent for showing us the area.

Sometime later, after we had gone back working on the Sandy Point Wreck, we returned to Fort Pierce and started making a magnetometer survey of the whole area there. Down the beach about a half mile from where he said it was, we found a cannon. And that was the so-called Colored Beach Wreck south of Fort Pierce, where we made this first big find of one point six million.

First the state got their twenty-five percent, the finders got their five percent, then Kip and I split the rest. And that was pretty fair. Even so these individuals got more than we did as individuals. And they did not have to do anything. But they did take us to the area. It ended up pretty fair. Then later on we made a settlement with them and paid them off completely, and they did not have any more interest in that area.

If that area was not in Wagner's search contract with the state, what happened?

Well, we hauled in that first batch of treasure and put it in the bank in Vero Beach. At that time the state did not have any archives board or any special department handling the stuff. It was being handled by a professor and a couple of his staff in Gainesville.

That night, when we brought the first big batch in, we invited Kip, all his men, and this professor from the university over to my house and told them we had something good to show them. They wanted to know if there was anything yellow in it and I said, "Yep." So they all came over, I gave them a drink and said, "Now I'm going to show you what we're finding." I opened up a pouch with a little gold nugget in it that I had found out in California and I said, "See here."

Kip didn't want to sound disappointed. He said, "Oh, that's really pretty." Then we opened up a couple more big piles with great big gold disks, seven and a half pounds each, and thousands of gold coins. It was really something to celebrate.

Someone told the governor that we had found a treasure, so he sent down a highway patrolman to investigate to see if someone had found a treasure without reporting it. The governor did not know that the university was handling this treasure hunting contract.

When we saw this guy spying on us we said, "Hey, you don't have to spy around. Whatever you want to know just ask us." He said, "Well you don't have any contract to dig this up." I said, "Sure we do. Kip Wagner's got the contract, and we've got a fifty-fifty contract with him."

He checked it out and said, "Yes, he has a contract, but it does not go far enough." So they extended his search area on down about another five miles past the wreck we had found, and they changed his contract to make it all legal.

Tell me how you divided the treasure.

Well, originally it was very fair and very easy. Kip couldn't make it there on the day we were dividing, so the others left it up to me and the state trooper to divide the treasure fairly. The fairest way we could think of was to divide it up just like us kids used to divide up a pie or cake. I cut the pieces of pie, and then the other guys got first choice to try and get the biggest piece of

The careful work of underwater archaeologist Carl J. Clausen to record precisely where each artifact was recovered on the site of the 1715 Cabin Wreck near Sebastian Inlet resulted in this over-all view of the dispersal pattern. Evidence indicates the vessel probably split its hull on the limestone ridge, resulting in a loss of ballast and treasure as the wreckage was swept shoreward in a westerly direction.

pie. We did the same thing. I divided the treasure into four piles that I figured were equal. I made sure that they were as equal as I could get them, because I gave the representative of the state, the trooper, first choice.

Were you separating the coins from the artifacts, or was this all coins?

No, we did the coins, the odd coins, separately. The gold coins were all sorted out, put on cards, and rated as to date, size, and mint and very evenly, fairly divided. Like if there were twelve gold doubloons all dated 1714, then the state got three and we got nine. Very fair.

With the artifacts, it was more difficult. Just by eyeballing the stuff we put them in four big even piles. The silver coins we divided by weight. We weighed them up and divided them in that manner.

You did not try to check out dates or anything? They had not been cleaned, had they?

No, not the silver coins. We just weighed them on a scale and divided them by weight. At first glance it may sound unreasonable, but not when you get to thinking about it. As long as we took these various sacks of coins, dumped out approximately one fourth of them from each sack into the state's pile, and weighed them, then everyone had a good random selection of coins.

Normally the division would be when—at the end of a dive season?

Yes. I would say the first division was great. We finished in the middle of June, and in July we had a division. That was terrific. That way we could sell some coins and operate.

We divided with the state, and then we kept finding treasure every year since then. For the last ten years we've averaged about a million bucks worth a year. And then last year, the last five months of seventy-three, we averaged about a million dollars worth a month. And right now we've got all our boats being overhauled and rebuilt during the windy, rough wintertime, and May first we plan to triple up the operation and work the *Atocha,* the *Margarita,* and another wreck we call the Mystery Wreck which is probably a British merchantman or a pirate ship.

4 〜〜〜

THE TROUBLE WITH TREASURE

In the spring of 1963, Albert Ashley and James Gordy, two young Florida skin divers, were diving for crawfish a few hundred yards offshore opposite the old Indian River Inlet near Fort Pierce, when they saw something on the bottom that made them forget all about crawfish. Scattered over the tops of the low Anastasia limestone formations paralleling the beach in this area were hundreds of gold coins, glittering as bright as the day they were minted. No Spanish treasure this, these were American gold coins dated 1857.

James Gordy's father, a Fort Pierce citrus grower, contacted the trustees of Florida's Internal Improvement Fund and obtained a lease on July 2, 1964, to salvage the coins.

The men worked the site from July to September 1964. Many times during this period, state underwater archaeologist Carl Clausen dived with them and was impressed by the simplicity of their operation. They would go out in their small fishing boat with sandwiches and bottled drinks, anchor in twelve feet of water, and dive up thousands of dollars worth of gold coins daily. And they continued to do this every day throughout the summer.

The coins recovered that year were found in an area measuring roughly fifty by eighty feet. Most were concentrated in small depressions in the surface of the reef, where the divers simply fanned away the light covering of sand to expose them. A few were wedged in rock crevices and had to be removed with padded needle-nose pliers to avoid scarring the coins. Others lay in deeper limestone pockets and were uncovered with a small injection dredge that "vacuumed" away the sand and loose shell. In this manner they recovered 477 one-, two-and-a-half-, five-, ten-, and twenty-dollar gold pieces, plus several hundred half dollars, quarters, and half dimes,* in less than three months. In addition the salvagers turned over to the state 105 other gold coins that they had salvaged from the site prior to the issuance of their lease, bringing their total reported find to 582 gold coins with a face value of $3,867 and a sale value at that time of $38,670.

When they found no more coins, the men stopped work, and in September 1964, the customary 75–25 percent division of the treasure was made between the state and the salvagers.

The matter might have rested there except for two possibly predictable circumstances—an archaeologist's curiosity and a falling out between the salvagers.

Clausen, curious about how the American gold coins got where they were found, wrote letters to Bruce Catton and other historians in an effort to pick up a lead to the puzzle. One of his queries led to a Florida newspaper man with a penchant for history. Two years after the find, the reporter mentioned a historical incident in an article he wrote. This was the clue Clausen was looking for. Following it up, the archaeologist searched microfilms of old Charleston newspapers and eventually tracked down the last detail of the event in the National Archives. Here is what he learned:

The Third Seminole War, which officially started with the

---

* Originally called a "half disme" by a 1792 law authorizing this denomination, the half dime was replaced by the nickel five-cent piece after 1866.

These American gold coins comprising part of a $230,000 army pay-roll lay exposed on the ocean bottom in eleven feet of water for eighty-eight years until found by two young scuba divers. Their reward was to share in the $230,000 rare-coin value of the find. By law, Florida retained 25 percent of the treasure. (Courtesy Carl Clausen)

not entirely unprovoked attack by Indians on a government survey party near Fort Myers in late December 1855, was in its seventeenth month when Major Jeremiah Yellot Dashiell of the army paymaster corps arrived off the Indian River Inlet on the east coast of Florida on May 1, 1857. Entrusted to Dashiell was a leather pouch containing $23,000 in gold, which had been withdrawn a few days earlier from the sub-treasury in Charleston, South Carolina. The money was intended for disbursement to federal troops in the major's pay district, which encompassed the Indian River area.

The major's primary objective was to reach Ford Capron on the west bank opposite the Indian River Inlet, where army troops were actively engaged in scouting the area for hostile Indians. Captain Cannon, master of the schooner *William and Mary* on which Dashiell had arrived, chose to anchor outside the inlet, which was noted at the time for its narrow channel and shifting sandbars. The major, his young son—who had accompanied him from Charleston—and four others disembarked in a small boat for the trip through the inlet to the fort. According to a Captain Nye who witnessed the accident from his schooner anchored inside the inlet, Major Dashiell's boat "was struck by a sea" when near the outer breakers and upset. Captain Nye manned a rescue boat that picked up all six persons, but the payroll was lost. All attempts to find the money were unsuccessful, for the bottom of the inlet in that area was described as quicksand. Congress later absolved Major Dashiell for any responsibility in the loss.

When Clausen told Ashley and the Gordys that he had learned that the lost payroll was $23,000, he wondered why their response was so lackadaisical.

The reason became apparent in 1968 when Ashley sued the Gordys for an accounting of the treasure and assets of the company. During this civil action, information was filed which indicated that the salvagers had misrepresented the size of their recovery by failing to report 2,600 additional gold coins that they had brought up in 1963. They had, in fact, found virtually all of Dashiell's payroll—with a face value of $23,025.50* and an actual sale value then of $230,255.

On April 18, 1968, the state of Florida filed suit against Ashley and the Gordys to recover the state property that they had illegally salvaged and disposed of. Four years later, the suit was settled in favor of the state.

And what happened to Major Dashiell after the loss? Unfortunately his bad luck continued. He withdrew an additional $28,000 in gold from the sub-treasury at Charleston to replace the lost funds, but on his return to Florida, $13,000 of this payroll was taken from his unattended baggage at a hotel in Palatka. Dashiell borrowed money to make up the deficit and pay the troops. Four months later, while he was at home in Texas trying to sell his property to pay off his debt, he learned that the marshall of Palatka had recovered $3,000 of his money from the hotel pro-

* $25.50 was either someone's pocket money or possibly left over from another payroll.

prietor's slave. Dashiell returned there but was unable to recover any more of the gold. The matter came up in Washington, where the secretary of war referred the case to President Buchanan, who recommended Dashiell's dismissal from the service. Dashiell was relieved of duty on July 10, 1858. His twelve years' service in the United States Army, begun during the war with Mexico, had ended, but Dashiell's military career was not finished.

He served as a colonel and inspector general for the state of Texas during the Civil War and returned after the war to San Antonio. A year before his death on March 14, 1888, Dashiell applied to Washington for a pension on the basis of his Mexican War service, but his pension was denied on the basis of the president's action.

More trouble with treasure started in May 1965 after a news story headlined "St. Petersburg 'Seven' Claim Rich Strike—Gulf Treasure Found" appeared in the *St. Petersburg Times.*

Times staff writer Dick Bothwell went on to describe the discovery of "a Spanish treasure find of major importance comparable to the notable Real Eight strike on Florida's east coast in the Spring of 1964. . . ." This was supposedly found about ninety miles south of St. Petersburg in the Gulf of Mexico off Florida's west coast. Bothwell's interview with John Sykes, spokesman for a group of St. Petersburg treasure hunters calling themselves the Lucky Seven revealed these details:

Sykes, who had been treasure hunting the Florida west coast for about eight years, said that he and his companions (whom he would not name) had located the wreck more than a year previous in water so shallow that "coins could be picked up while wading." They were looking for something else and had discovered the wreck by accident. Apparently the vessel had burned to the waterline, because they found nails twisted and melted from the heat. Several feet of sand that would have to be moved covered the wreck. Probing revealed buried ship's timbers, and the treasure hunters' sand dredges turned up coral-encrusted coins and artifacts. Sykes said his group had applied for a salvage permit from the state about two months before the east coast strike but it was

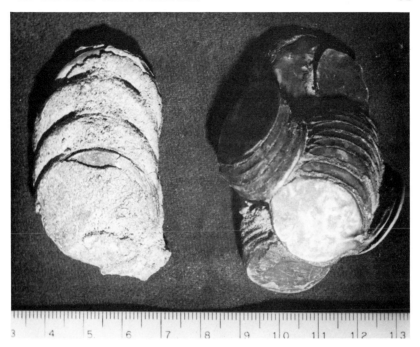

*United States silver coins recovered from site 8-UW-5 located north of
Fort Pierce inlet. They were part of the American gold payroll lost
in 1857 and found by divers in 1963.* (Courtesy Carl Clausen)

being held up. Now he felt pretty sure that it would be issued.

When archaeologist Clausen learned of the Gulf find, he flew
to St. Petersburg with the state's field investigator, Philip Thibedeau, to examine and catalog the treasure. Then, in accordance
with state policy, it was to be locked in safe deposit boxes at the
First Federal Savings and Loan Association's office there. According to Bothwell's news story, the items consisted of "three Aztec
figurines five to six inches tall, two of gold, one bronze; an Aztec
sacrificial sword, with blade of bronze and hilt of silver; and a
number of coins, mostly silver pieces of eight. Many bear the date
1698, and come from the Mexico City mint."

A fact some readers may have missed in their eagerness to get
to the juicier part of Bothwell's article, was a statement by inves-

tigator Philip Thibedeau: "The state has begun an investigation to check [the treasure's] authenticity," he said. "There are some points of conflict with the coins found on the east coast."

This was the understatement of the day. As soon as Clausen saw the find he was skeptical. He was quite familiar with pre-Columbian metal castings from Mexico, Central, and South America, and these did not look like Indian workmanship. Furthermore, the coins were crude castings instead of being struck, as were authentic coins from the New World mints of that period.

Wallace Minto, a Sarasota metallurgical expert who had been shown the finds before the state confiscated them, said, "The sword intrigued me the most. Although I didn't have an opportunity to touch it, several flaws were evident. The blade was not steel. It was either bronze or copper. They [the treasure hunters] said it was bronze. Bronze swords have not been used since the time of the Romans. It was too soft. The hilt of the sword was shaped in the form of a Teutonic cross, which the Spaniards never used and the Germans have used only in modern times. The cross looked very much like a mail-order advertisement of a few years ago for an SS officer's knife."

Minto's observations on the other artifacts were equally revealing. "The figurines were not gold," he said, "but gold-plated in a modern style called bright gold. They were also castings. The art of casting was not developed by the Aztecs. [Here Minto was either incorrect or misquoted by the newspaper.] The specific gravity was such that I believe these to be brass. The figurines themselves, I am certain, were bookends you could buy through the mail from Mexico a few years ago."

Details of the attempted fraud became clearer when Clausen examined discrepancies in the silver coins Sykes had turned over to the state for cataloging. Of course the most obvious flaw to even an untrained expert's eye was that the coins had been cast, a process that the Spanish had not used in making their early coins. Instead, they cut them from poured strips of silver with chisels or hand shears, clipped them to legal weight, then stamped them between steel dies. This generally gave the coins a slightly convex face, the obverse, with two rounded sides from the original poured

Closeup of United States silver coin dated 1857 lost near Fort Pierce with a Federal payroll intended for troops fighting the Third Seminole War in Florida. (Courtesy Carl Clausen)

strip and two sharp sides where they had been cut off (unless the coin represented either end of the original poured strip in which case it would have only one cut side). The cast counterfeits had straight sharp edges all around. Also, pure Spanish silver was generally so soft that authentic coins could usually be marked with a fingernail. But the fake coins were too hard to be scratched. Under magnification some of the counterfeits revealed file marks—an unmistakable indication that the coins were bogus.

Less obvious to most coin experts, however, were discrepancies Clausen found in details on the faces of the coins. For instance, one series of fake eight-real pieces were marked with the date 1711, but the crest or royal shield shown on the coin belonged to a period seventy-five years earlier. A bead from a portion of a decorative semicircle was missing. Clausen knew this could happen in genuine coins when there was a defect in the Spaniard's die, but he also knew that two silver coins from the same die were very seldom encountered. Yet the same defect appeared on all the fake coins in the series. Certain areas of the coins had an unnatural smoothness, as if defective high spots may have been ground overly smooth in the counterfeiting process. Mint marks on the forgeries were OM, with F, the initial of the royal assayer. This was the

This crudely made counterfeit coin from the phony Gulf Galleon betrays itself by the manner in which it is made. The coin was cast, instead of cut from a bar. The letter "F" for the Mexico City mint assayer is incorrect and the overall crudity of the design stamps this as a very poor imitation. (Courtesy Carl Clausen) *Right: Closeup shows sticklike figures in counterfeit coin said found on the phony Gulf Galleon. Although original Spanish silver coins were made without refinement, they were far better than this.* (Courtesy Carl Clausen)

Mexico City mint. But in 1711 the mark was OXM plus the assayer's initial, which was *not* F, but J. Assayer F did not appear until several years later. The lack of symmetry and a notch in the outline of the coin's embossed shield indicated the counterfeiter's carelessness. The most glaring example of this was within the shield design itself. On a genuine piece of eight, two small areas in the crest represented the Lion of Flanders and the Eagle of the Tyrol. In these same places, the counterfeit contained only meaningless marks. Unfortunately, however, the poor quality of the forgeries was still good enough to fool collectors who knew little or nothing about early Spanish coins.

To further complicate matters, authorities learned that the fraudulent Gulf galleon silver pieces represented a fraction of several hundred of these counterfeit coins already circulating. Most were eight reals but there were others of smaller denominations. An indeterminate number of sets containing one, two, four, and eight reals had been sold to coin collectors along the Treasure

Coast. Clausen knew of such sets that had been sold for $140. One coin dealer in Fort Pierce even tried to sell sets of the counterfeits after it had been brought to his attention that they were fakes. Considering that each set could have been manufactured for less than five dollars, it was a lucrative business.

Obviously the counterfeiters were capitalizing on the genuine finds from the 1715 wrecks off the Florida east coast. Real Eight and Treasure Salvors were in no way involved with the counterfeits. They had too many real coins to bother with fakes. Clausen and other state officials, nevertheless, hastened to reassure coin collectors that these companies were "very much above board, very honest and very legal" in selling their original coins. Clausen felt that the only fair thing to do was to point out the difference between the counterfeits and the authentic coins in newspapers and various trade journals so that these two companies would not be harmed when marketing their merchandise. Detailed articles comparing the real and counterfeit Spanish colonial coins appeared in issues of *Coin World*, the weekly newspaper of the numismatic field.

Clausen turned over all the accumulated evidence of the counterfeit-coin fraud to the local Florida state attorney's office, but clamping down on the forgers and making the charges stick proved to be something else again. The counterfeiter could swear in court that he never represented the coins as genuine, and the dealer could testify that he was taken in, that he was also a victim. But whether the counterfeits were bought for trading or as an investment, they still represented possible disillusion and financial embarrassment to the dealer.

Gold fever knows no boundaries. It strikes young and old, rich or poor, professional treasure hunter or armchair enthusiast alike. For the unwary, it can be disastrous.

In 1970 a retired citrus grower asked Clausen to look at some treasure items he had recently purchased as an investment. Clausen went to south Florida and the man showed him the most amazing collection of "treasure" he had ever seen—80 percent of it fake.

"It was almost as bad as the things that supposedly turned up on the west coast's phony Gulf galleon," said Clausen. "There was just enough authentic stuff to carry the day. The rest was junk." It included almost two hundred gold and silver coins dated into the early eighteenth century, a golden dragon whistle valued at $50,000, a gold ring and necklace, twelve small gold bars, and an equal number of silver bars.

"This was no fly-by-night twenty-thousand-dollar deal," said Clausen. "Enormous amounts of money and extremely valuable property such as motels had changed hands in this transaction. The old man had given fifty thousand dollars for a fake dragon pendant like that specimen recovered by Real Eight. His total investment in the 'treasure' was between four hundred thousand and five hundred thousand dollars. He had bought it because one day he thought it would be super-valuable—and all he was holding was a bunch of fakes."

Where had it come from? Clausen learned that two men had offered it to the old man as authentic treasure, reportedly part of Kip Wagner's share of the Real Eight-Treasure Salvors' finds. The grower had in turn showed it to a supposedly reputable treasure hunter who, intentionally or otherwise, failed to point out that most of it was fake. Only after the transaction had taken place had the citrus grower's wife become suspicious about her husband's investment and encouraged him to have the collection appraised by someone with a knowledge of Spanish colonial coins and artifacts. As a result, after examining the collection, Clausen had the unenviable task of telling the retired couple that they were the victims of an elaborate fraud that had apparently bilked them out of almost half a million dollars.

Now that's *real* treasure trouble!

5 〰

Tom Gurr: Curse of the San José

Tom Gurr is one of the most likeable rogues I know. Tall, husky, bushy-bearded, usually wearing only swimming trunks and a red stocking cap to work, he looks every inch the buccaneer he surely would have been in an earlier century. Today, however, he is a professional treasure hunter, one who over the years has carried on an almost self-annihilating love affair with a 243-year-old Spanish shipwreck. Old documents list the vessel as the *San Joseph y las Animas*, more affectionately known as the *San José*, formerly of the ill-fated Spanish treasure fleet destroyed by a hurricane in the Florida Straits in 1733. Tom found her, along with the remains of her treasure, and inherited what some say was the curse of the *San José*.

I first met Tom on his salvage boat *El Capitan* out of Islamorada a few years before this interview. We dived together on the ballast-laden skeleton of the *San José* and searched for treas-

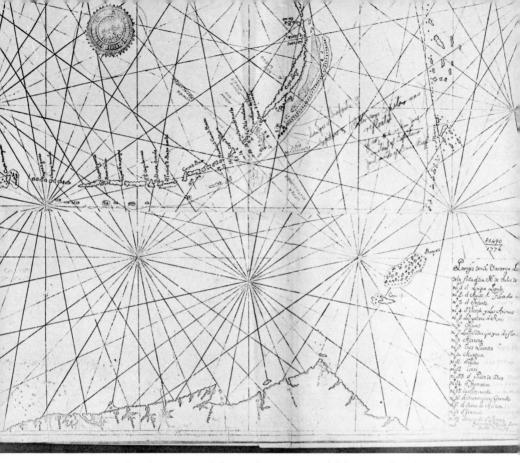

Reproduction of an eighteenth-century British map that is a copy of a Spanish map showing the locations of wrecks of the Spanish fleet destroyed in the Florida Keys by a hurricane in 1733. The handwritten notes of treasure hunters can be seen on the document. (Courtesy Carl Clausen)

ure. In those days Tom's problems had not yet grown totally out of proportion, but the storm warnings were on the horizon. While few coins were coming off the wreck, I remember how happy he was to recover a richly decorated Oriental ginger jar. It was not the rarity of the item that pleased him so much as the knowledge that this fragile piece of porcelain had traveled from China to the Philippines, crossed the Pacific on the Manila galleon to Acapulco, negotiated the mountains of Mexico on a mule train to Vera Cruz, was loaded aboard a ship of the *Flota* that sailed the circuitous treasure route to Havana, survived a hurricane that demolished the ship on its journey to Spain, and somehow endured the next 240 years on the bottom of the ocean until the day he found it, completely unscathed and intact.

Being a part of this minor miracle meant more to Tom than finding a fistful of silver coins. But long-lived ginger jars did not put bread on the table or pay his boat's fuel bill. And this was the crux of the problem. Tom's wreck produced more non-negotiable artifacts than gold or silver. Moreover, he was trapped by a bureaucratic system that squeezed him into an intolerable position, then left him to languish until he reacted in the only way he knew how. In retrospect one may criticize the man's method of reacting, but it might also do well to question the proprieties of the system that provided the catalyst for those reactions.

This interview took place at a treasure hunting friend's apartment not far from the turtle *kraals* on a warm sunny August afternoon in Key West. Tom was wearing a shortsleeved sport shirt imprinted with a design of small anchors. A handsome piece of eight hung from a silver chain at his neck. The following day, he and his attorney, David H. Horan, were to appear in court to answer the state charges of grand larceny. Tom cheerfully looked forward to his day in court, his long-anticipated day of retribution.

Tell me something about your background, Tom, and how you got into the treasure hunting business.

Well, I was born in St. Augustine on December 11, 1928. I guess maybe being raised around all that history got me interested in it. I went to school in Jacksonville, and just after World War II, I joined the navy and volunteered for the underwater demolition team, which was the big thing then.

After training, our team was sent to Bikini for Operation Crossroads, the atomic bomb tests there and at Eniwetok. I got out of the service in late 1949, and since all my friends and my brothers were in it, I joined an air national guard outfit with the rank of staff sergeant, the equivalent of my navy rank of petty officer second class.

I was doing fine. Had a new job as an insurance investigator, got married in May 1959, my wife was pregnant along about July, and then the Koreans upset things.

After being out of the service for about nine months, I was recalled. That ninety-day callup for the national guard stretched into three years in Korea, where I received a field commission to provost marshall in the Air Force.

After coming home, I got my first two years in college and was the Civil Defense coordinator of seven southeast Georgia counties. When it looked like I was to be transfered to Gila Bend, Arizona, which didn't appeal to me, I resigned my commission and got into the building business with my family in Jacksonville. In 1960 I went back to college and studied engineering. Then in 1962 I went with the Florida Flood Control District where I was made field engineer for Dade County.

I guess I was one of the first diving engineers that Florida had. This was a new state agency, and they were just putting it together. I trained a six-man diving team to work with me, and we did surveys, underwater inspections, underwater maintenance, repairs, *et cetera* on state maintained locks and dams. Since we lived in Miami just off from some of the finest diving waters in the world, this is where I got involved. I bought a thirty-two-foot Owens cabin cruiser, and it was not long before my wife and myself and the whole crew I had trained were out diving on a weekend. Pretty soon we got interested in treasure hunting, because that was the big thing down there. We found some nice things in 1964.

Had you done any prior to that as a young man?

Not other than just kicking around the beaches and collecting arrowheads, pottery shards, and this sort of thing. As a youngster we lived west of St. Augustine and I roamed the woods a lot. Up around Jacksonville, going to school when I was a teenager, we were some of the first kids to find old Fort Caroline. We found it when it was overgrown with vines and bushes. We packed in with a Boy Scout outfit and spent weekends doing a lot of digging and searching for old artifacts. So I guess the early historical influence went back as far as that.

But you started treasure hunting after you got your boat?

Yes, this would be the first real involvement. We were two or three hundred yards off Elliot Key on one of our first trips, and we had anchored near the Cement Barrel Wreck, a barge that had gone down with a load of cement that had hardened and looked like cordwood stacked up on the barge. It was loaded with fish and in about twelve feet of water. In swimming around that area weekend after weekend, we strayed off and found an old ballast pile. In fact, after several months we found three ballast piles right offshore close to Elliot Key. I got interested in old Black Caesar, the pirate, because this was really his area. Black Caesar's Creek was there, and we got to digging into the history and hunting everything we could find about him.

Actually we found that Adam's Key was possibly where he had his harem. It's either myth or history, because there is little known about it. We found a lot of things on the key and in the shallow waters around it to indicate that there were women on the island during an early period. We found lipstick cases of early decorated brass, ivory combs—this type of thing. More or less we were trying to prove that there was such a person as Black Caesar. Of course, the story has it that he would careen his ship behind this island in Black Caesar's Creek to keep his masts down below

Looking every inch the swashbuckling rogue of another century, Captain Tom Gurr added a little spice to the sometimes humdrum profession of treasure hunting when he called in the TV cameras and threw all of the state-owned treasure he had found back into the ocean. Or so it seemed.

the mangroves, and then when a fat Spanish galleon came by he'd cut the lines, spring up, and sail out in his fast ship to capture it. Then he would bring the prize into shore, loot the vessel, take all the women off, kill all the men, and burn and scuttle the ship. I think this was the reason for all the ballast piles.

On Ajax Reef we found some blockade runners. Then on north Key Largo, we worked on the *Winchester*, which is a pretty well known wreck—and the old Piller Dollar Wreck, which was just north of that. It more or less evolved, one thing led to another.

Had you built any air lifts yet?

Yes, we used an air lift that I had from the early days. We were working with that when the Real Eight find was made in 1964. That really gave us a shot of enthusiasm.

You were still with the Flood Control then?

Yes, I was with them until the last part of 1966. I treasure hunted on weekends. We got deeper into it as we went along, and then I applied while I was still with Flood Control. When the state imposed a moratorium on treasure hunting in Florida waters, I went outside the three-mile limit and stayed out there to work. When the moratorium went off, I applied for a state salvage license on one of the wreck sites. But considering the paper work, the red tape, and everything involved, I couldn't see any advantage of working with the state. So I sent the application back and said no thanks.

Did you have any particular wreck site offshore that you were interested in at that time?

Yes, I was still working those Elliot Key wrecks—the Black Caesar stuff, because we had gotten a few goodies off them that Black Caesar may not have liked, but we did. They were brass name plates, a few coins, and interesting artifacts.

What kind of coins?

English, dated 1800, and I think we got some Portuguese Joes, whatever they are. But I gave them all away over a period of time. We had a small operation and didn't want to put a lot of money into it, but the state required this. So I stayed outside the state waters. And we got involved as we got into the lower keys.

This huge anchor standing outside a restaurant in the Florida Keys proved incapable of holding its vessel against the fury of sea and hurricane. The relic, with ballast rocks still encrusted on its flukes, once belonged to one of the ill-fated galleons of the 1733 fleet. It was but one of several such giant anchors carried by the great ships.

We got onto the *Infante*, for instance, which was pretty good. At that point—it was late 1966—I worked myself out of a job, you might say.

When I first went with Flood Control, I was in the field all the time diving with the men, but then I became a desk jockey. I trained my people too well apparently. But I sat behind a desk eight to five, five days a week, bumper-to-bumper traffic, to work in the morning and home at night. I couldn't cut it. I found myself sitting in the office staring at the walls Monday morning waiting for Friday to come. Finally I made up my mind that this was not for me. So I called up my wife one day and said, "Hey, I just sent in my letter of resignation." She said, "What are you going to do?" I said, "We're going treasure hunting." Instead of blowing her stack she said, "Great." We owned a private school in Coconut Grove and had a little money saved, so I figured this was the time to do it. This is when we got the old *Parker* from up on

Closeup view of galleon anchor fluke shows egg ballast rock welded by sea and time to the iron. Such anchors were sometimes jettisoned at the last moment in the hope of lightening the ship enough for it to ride over the reefs to ground nearer shore.

Miami River where she was sunk at dockside there.

What was her background?

She was built in 1882 as a New York pilot boat, a twin-masted sailing schooner that worked up there until 1935, when they retired her. Someone picked up the hull, converted her to diesel, and she hauled freight on the Chesapeake as a lugger from 1935 to 1966, when Captain Mole out of Key Largo bought her. The hull was still sound, so he built a bigger cabin on her and was going to bring her to the Keys as a houseboat. But in trying to bring the vessel through some of the shallow channels, he grounded her and knocked off the rudder and screw. When the Coast Guard tried to pull her free, it ripped off the keel, deadwood and all. So that was her condition when we got her. I bought the hull for fifteen hundred dollars. Then, with some of my original divers who had quit the Flood Control with me, we started converting her.

We rebuilt the boat and put booms on her. A surplus air compressor, air hoses, and lengths of twenty-one-foot-long eight-inch diameter aluminum irrigation tubes became our air lifts. We could run three eight-inch air lifts with a six hundred cfm compressor. Pressure was no problem here. It was the volume. We bought a surplus fifty-six cfm navy diving compressor, and we could run six divers in Desco rigs comfortably off it. We had a beautiful rig there, three hundred feet of hose for each diver.

Had you formed a company at that time?

No, at that time I was still on my own. I footed most of the bills. This was in 1967. We formed the company in March 1968. I carried the load pretty much by myself, selling things as we pulled them up, which was the natural thing for a treasure hunter to do. You go out, recover something, and you need money to operate so you sell it and get more money to put into it. It's like any business; you have to be able to turn your merchandise. This was the method we used through 1967. We worked areas like Coffins Patch off Marathon, and we did fairly well on the old *San Fernando*. We got a few coins and artifacts off it—things like flintlock pistols and arquebuses—that we could sell.

This was outside the three-mile limit?

Yes, I refused to work within the three-mile limit. I didn't want the hassle with the state. I had had enough of the red tape with government agencies in the service and with the Flood Control, so I purposely stayed outside. This was the way we worked. In fact we went over to the Bahamas and worked on the *Maravilla* site and got some fringe areas of that. Bob Marx will love me for that, because I actually gave Bob some overlays of some charts we had up there when he decided to go over.

But I got discouraged in the Bahamas because a real good friend of mine had said, "Look, I don't want you to come out here with the idea that you will be able to make it and be able to walk away. The Bahamian government is not going to let any American walk away with anything out of the Bahamas." It seems that somebody had gotten over there earlier and rooked them out of some coins or something. Anyway, they were down on Americans. So, we left the Bahamas with whatever we had. I told Bob all this, but he didn't believe me. Later he found out I was right.

Anyway, this was our operation. Mel Fisher and I got together about late 1967. He had finished up the season in Vero Beach and was moving into the Keys to look for the *Atocha*. We needed the use of a magnetometer, because we had worked all the visible wrecks, scavenging on wrecks that other people had found. So I hooked up with Mel and we had an agreement. Since we had a full crew and a well equipped heavy-duty salvage boat, we would work the incidental wrecks that he found as a result of looking for the *Atocha*.

On shares?

Yes, it was a good arrangement. We found a couple virgin wrecks that turned out quite well. One of them was the Blunder-buss Wreck. In the summer of 1968, when Mel left to go back to his operation at Vero Beach, I talked him into leaving his mag with me. I had learned to operate it from watching Fay Fields and Dick Williams use it, so I knew I could do it safely. Williams stayed down with me for a couple weeks in June, and we started searching, using the old Spanish chart that everyone else had.

Of the 1733 fleet?

Right. The old Spanish salvor's chart. It had everything pretty well located, and the thing that interested me was that every wreck on the chart was accurate to within three quarters of a mile of the actual wrecks that had already been found. In fact I had found no real variations. The *Infante*, the *Capitana*, the *Herrera*, the *Tres Puentes*—all of these wrecks surrounded the place where the *San José* was supposed to be. But nobody had found it yet. I got the idea that if we started working in this particular area and did a grid sweep with the mag, we were going to run across it.

So we started at about Conch Buoy and came into what we estimated was the three-mile limit and put our markers up. Then we started gridding it out at about one hundred foot intervals and magged our way south. We just worked back and forth and on the third day, boom, we hit it! That's how accurate that thing was. Of course, as soon as we hit it we called the big boat over, started digging, and found that we had a real old virgin. We knew pretty well what we had because of the ballast stone and the timbers.

Was it all covered at the time?

Yes, it had eel grass over it, which was something unusual. Most of the wrecks we had found were covered with sand. There would be a little patch of grass around them. But this wreck was completely covered with eel grass, and when we got the mag read-ing and went down and looked, you couldn't believe it. You learn, though, that if a mag says it's there you have faith in it, and you keep digging until you find it. But this was so unusual . . . when I went down there was grass everywhere I looked. I went back and said are we sure of this tape? We looked at it again and sure enough. Of course, we had cross-sectioned this thing to make damn sure that we did not get a false reading. We literally drew a picture of it with the magnetometer before we went down. But that grass was something else. It was thick. We had to dig down through about eighteen inches of root growth with our diving knives. After that, we went through two or three feet of soft sand and hit ballast rocks. Then we were looking at a wreck that hadn't been seen by a human for over two hundred years.

When I heard that Mendel Peterson of the Smithsonian Institution was in the area, I called him and told him that we had a real hot one that looked good. He got the Explorers Research Corporation to foot the bill for him and a crew to come down from the Smithsonian and the National Park Service. The latter had just gotten into underwater archaeology, and I guess had just trained George Fisher how to dive that year, so about ten or twelve people came down and started from Day One. Of course, we had to slow our pace down and they had to speed theirs up, but we had a meeting in the middle where they could get the data necessary—the mapping of the wreck, identifying and preserving the artifacts as they came up—and we could still maintain our salvage pace. There was a good working relationship there in those early days.

What were some of the early finds?

There were, of course, coins. They were some of the first things we got into right in the ballast stones and on the edge of the ballast. There were also onion bottles in the ballast. We'd find complete olive jars and never could understand why they were not broken, but we'd move ballast stones and here these things would be in there. We found a variety of items: a little glass cat from the Orient, about fifty or sixty gold rings, two gold coins, pistols, swords, a lot of personal things—some of them quite unusual. For instance, we found a wood cartridge belt. This updates history because they did not think cartridge belts were used until the Revolutionary War period, but here were the Spaniards using them back in 1733. That plus some Japanese porcelain that the Smithsonian expert identified. Others didn't agree with him. They said that wasn't possible because there was no trade with Japan until a hundred years later with Perry. So they sent it to this expert in New York and he concurred and said yes, it was Japanese porcelainware. Here it was, from an uncontaminated wreck site. That was absolute.

Was it K'ang-Hsi?

Yes, it was the K'ang-Hsi period, but this was Japanese in origin. It probably came by way of Macao and the Philippines, the same way as the Chinese porcelain, but the general concept was that Japan had no trade ties with the Western world until Admiral Perry. This was proof positive that a century before Perry there was a trade route into Japan.

These things were very interesting to me. I guess I got as interested in that as anything else. Some of the personal items you really get close to, you really feel for them. I used to tell the guys that I get turned on more by finding something like a piece of jewelry, a gold ring—something that had a personal connection, something you could relate to rather than just coins. Of course, I still get a thrill when I run into a pile of coins, you know. I still get the cold chill that runs up your back, but I think there are other items—one of a kind type of things—that give you just as much of a thrill. That's what we were finding out there.

Things went along well. Peterson left in August, and we carried on with the work and kept up with the correspondence. Some of the others stayed with us, too. By then, of course, we had formed a company [March 1968] just before the discovery. It was called Marine Tech. It was a small company, but it grew as we went along.

Were you having to keep the Parker *anchored over the site?*

Yes, since we were in international waters, four-point-two miles off the coast. I have a federal salvage license, which I acquired through the federal court in Miami—the same kind of license, incidentally, that the old wreckers here in Key West used to have. It was put on the books in 1847 to protect the wreck sites here because whenever a ship wrecked, everyone would rush for it

Treasure hunter and author Martin Meylach removes an unbroken olive jar from a 1733 Spanish shipwreck in the Florida Keys. These ceramic containers were used to carry a variety of comestibles aboard early Spanish sailing vessels. (Courtesy Martin Meylach)

and there was a lot of trouble. The first guy on the wreck was appointed master. But this loose arrangement resulted in so many arguments, fights, and killings that the federal government put a law into effect that said all salvage masters had to be licensed. They then had to divide their spoils with whoever helped them work the wrecks. This law is still good and is required in federal waters outside our three-mile limit.

Did you get the license after you found the San José?

No, I got it in 1967. Somebody had told me that if I found anything, to be completely legal, which I wanted to do, I needed the license. When I checked I found this was true. So I got the license and I still carry it. At that time only two others were in existence. Unless you do something to have it revoked, it is always good.

So I was master of the vessel and I was licensed by the federal government as a salvage master in international waters, but yet that did not give me any privileges as far as protection for the site. So the only thing I could do to protect it was get something big enough to stay out there. Of course the ninety-foot *Parker* was big enough, and I had a crew that knew how to take care of themselves, so we were pretty safe from that standpoint. This was our activity, then. Things would be salvaged, we needed money, so we would sell them and put the money back into the company for operating expenses.

This went along good until late October or November 1968, when a couple of state agents came out and wanted to board the boat. Of course we wouldn't allow it because we were a documented vessel in international waters where the state of Florida had no jurisdiction. So we told them, "Hell no, get away."

One of the guys made the error of trying to come aboard anyway, but a couple of shots in the water turned him away. They high-tailed it back to the beach, and I guess they were kind of mad because they apparently called Carl Clausen, the state archaeologist overseeing Florida's treasure salvage program at that time. Clausen apparently got mad, too, and called the customs department in Miami to report that he had information about a boat being used by the CIA to drop off guns and ammunition for Cuban refugees making raids on Cuba. He described our boat by name and everything.

The next day we got a visit from a forty-foot Coast Guard cutter. It came alongside with five civilians armed with Thompson submachine guns. They went through the motions of jacking rounds into the chambers of their weapons and said, "We're boarding you." I said, "Yes, sir."

We backed up and they put us against the bulkhead with our hands in the air. A couple agents stood guard while the others went below and made a full search of the boat.

Of course they didn't find anything. They registered the serial numbers of every weapon, but we were legal. We were allowed to have one firearm per crew member, as long as it was not an automatic weapon. We even had a twenty-millimeter antitank gun. It was legal because it was a single shot. And one of the agents said, "Is that really necessary?" I said, "Well, you never know." Anyway they left us and I couldn't get any explanation of what the hell they were doing there. I was real hopping mad about that time.

After the Coast Guard left, I got back on the beach and called the Coast Guard commander at Key West, but he refused to give me any information. Next I started with the local chief in Islamorada, and he referred me to command. Then I went to Seventh District Coast Guard and tried to get the admiral. He wasn't available, but I got into the legal department and he said, "No, you're mistaken. It wasn't a Coast Guard vessel. We haven't done that since prohibition days." I said, "Well, you just did it today."

They referred me back and forth and finally a lieutenant in the legal department called me back and said he had found out what it was. He said the Coast Guard was not involved. They had furnished transportation for the customs people at their request. I didn't get much satisfaction out of them. They just said, "Well, you know, it's all been resolved so let's forget it." I said, "Forget it, hell. You boarded my vessel at gun point, harassed my crew, and stopped our operations and I want an explanation." They refused to give it to me, so I got ahold of Dante Fascell, our local representative, and I said, "Look, I don't know if we're living in Russia or not, but this is what just happened to me."

Two days later I got an official apology from the commander of the Seventh District Coast Guard. The customs people told me that they had made a mistake and that they had acted irrationally without first checking it out. So this was sort of a get-even scheme. Clausen and I laugh about it now when we get together, but then we both did a few things to each other which kind of evened things out.

This was our first encounter with the state. I thought that was it. Then about a week later I was going ashore because I had my family down in the Keys then and I commuted. The sheriff's department and the state agent, Phil Thibedeau, met me on the dock and handed me some papers when I stepped ashore. It was a summons to appear in a local Monroe County court in Key West.

Aboard his salvage vessel, El Capitan, *out of Islamorada, Florida, Captain Tom Gurr signals for the L-shaped blower pipe to be lowered over the ship's wheel during dredging operations on the wreck of the* San José.

I called the attorney and he said, "No sweat. The Constitution says what the boundaries are and we're in international waters. You got loran fixes of what your site is?" I said, "Yep. Even the Coast Guard verified that we were at four-point-two-eight miles off-shore." So we went to court and started fighting.

In the long weeks of bitter court fighting that followed, Tom Gurr fought a losing battle. The state's legal argument was based on Florida's constitution of 1865, which placed Florida's shoreline at her outermost reef. Therefore, Florida's territorial three-mile-limit in this area not only took in the *San José* but placed her jurisdictional boundary well out into the Gulf Stream. Ruling for the state, the circuit judge issued a temporary injunction preventing Gurr from any further excavation of the wreck.

Gurr's attorney took the case to the federal court, arguing that his client was operating legally under a federal salvage license and that Florida was overstepping her boundaries into federal waters.

Unfortunately, what Gurr and his attorney did not know was that Florida and twelve other states were about to enter a suit filed by the federal government to contest ownership of the submerged lands claimed by the states. While the Justice Department argued that the thirteen Atlantic coast states owned land only out to a distance of three miles, the states claimed much more. Florida's attorney general obviously realized that if a federal judgment could be secured affecting the states' jurisdiction over a shipwreck, thereby establishing a new point from which to measure the three-mile limit, it would strengthen the state's case in the upcoming suit.

Probably well aware of these facts, Miami's federal judge William Mehrtens refused to take the case.

The case was to be heard on January 6, 1969, but on December 23, 1968, I was summoned to the federal court in Miami, where Judge Mehrtens ordered me to obey the lower court order. I said, "I'm sorry, your honor, I don't understand." He said, "Maybe if you spend six months in Atlanta, you'll understand." And I said, "No sir, I think you've made your point clear."

You were then told to turn over all your recovered treasure to the state?

Yes. On January 6, I had to carry all the recovered treasure that was, as the court order said, "in [my] care, custody and control," and turn it over to the clerk of the federal court who gave me a receipt for it. That same day, ex-Senator Williams* approached me in the hall of the federal court and said, "Look, Tom, if you win a point we're going to appeal it and I'm sure you'll do the same thing. It could go back and forth and we could spend three years in litigation. The state is prepared to go all the way to the Supreme Court. You'll be out of operation and I'm

* Robert Williams, director of Florida's Division of Archives, History and Records Management, the department overseeing Florida's treasure salvage program.

certain you don't have the finances to do this. . . ."

I assured him that I did not have. I had already gone through a lot of money by this time. He appealed to my conscience, mentioning the damage being done to these wrecks with no one overseeing them. He said that if I would allow the lower court's order to stand and to drop all litigation and not challenge it, that the state would then enter into a contract with me to finish the *San José* and then give me an area of my choice of exploration.

So we were allowed to go back to work. We agreed that the federal clerk could release the material to the state, and we worked without the benefit of the contract up to and through the summer of 1969. I think it was about July that I got copies of the contracts and, man, they weren't anything near like what they had promised us. In fact they were so bad that we were only getting fifty percent instead of the customary seventy-five percent. They wrote in the contract that we were being penalized because we had caused the state expensive litigation.

Had this part been mentioned to you earlier?

Hell no, because we were working real happily. We had a state agent on board and no contract or anything—just this agreement we had worked out verbally because they were going to draw up the contracts. This was January, and it took us until July to even get copies of the contracts. So when I got them I flipped my lid. I called Williams on the phone and he as much as told me that that was the best terms we were going to get, to take them or leave them. I said, "well I won't take them." So he called down to his agent and ordered the operation shut down. Of course I didn't want to fight the whole battle over, but we pulled into Marathon, and here we went again. I got a lawyer and we headed for Tallahassee. In the little hassling that we had up there it was pretty well decided by my attorney that they had us over a barrel. He told me to accept what they offered and to go with it. Otherwise, I was out of business.

During this time the *Parker* sank at dockside in Marathon. I didn't have the money to pay my crew, because the state had collected our recoveries in December and January, and they had not given us a division. And here it was August. The money just ran

Holding a fragile K'ang-Hsi period Chinese porcelain ginger jar he found buried beside the wreck of the San José, *Captain Tom Gurr marvels that the piece withstood a trip halfway around the world and over two centuries of nature's ravages to survive intact.*

out. There was nothing to sell and I couldn't raise any more. When I couldn't pay the crew, they left and there was no one to take care of the boat. One day the power went off, the bilge pumps quit, and the boat just settled down in the mud and I lost her.

[Lacking boat, money, and a crew, Gurr finally agreed to the terms of the contract they wanted to give him. But without any funds or equipment, he was compelled to join forces with another treasure salvage firm. With the assistance of Bob Marx and the Real Eight Company's salvage boat, *Griffon,* he started working the wreck again. Three months later when Real Eight began having financial problems of its own, the work stopped again. Throughout this period Gurr repeatedly asked the state for the customary division of the recovered treasure that would give him the needed funds to continue work. But no division was forthcoming.]

What was the reason for this?

Their excuse was that they had no laboratory [a facility where artifacts could be kept, usually immersed in water to prevent deterioration until they could be properly preserved and cataloged.] They had one on the following year's budget, 1970. So when the budget went through and the laboratory was all set up, I said, "Okay, you've got the lab, how about a division?" They said, "Well, we don't have a preservationist. That was going to be in the next year's budget." This is the kind of runaround they gave me.

But they had been dividing with other treasure hunting firms?

Yes, with Real Eight Company and the others. But they told me the reason for that was because I was getting eighty or ninety percent artifacts, whereas the Real Eight Company got eighty or ninety percent coins while working other sites. In other words, "We need to study your material more. We need it better preserved."

Had the state agreed to split with you on the treasure that you had already found prior to the time they took it away from you?

They agreed verbally. They were to take all the stuff and the things that would not need to go through the process of study such as coins, jewelry, *et cetera*, things that had a commercial value, they were going to divide with me. They used the term *six months*. And of course when the contract thing came up about the same time as this it kind of blew the whole thing out of kilter you might say.

Did they want a salvage fee after all this?

According to our original deal, Williams agreed to waive the bond and the fee in our case since we had already salvaged it. They already had this material. But when the contract came, it demanded the original fee and the bond.

I called Williams on it and he said, "Well, we found by law that we couldn't do that," and I said, "That's too bad, because we worked this whole summer on the assumption that you could. Also, the area that I had applied for for exploration was fifty square miles, but when they sent it back it was only eighteen." Williams said that by law they could only give us eighteen and I said, "Why did you promise me fifty? Don't promise me what you can't deliver." And this was the kind of hot argument we had.

This was all relative to the San José?

Yes, in fact there were five people sitting in the attorney general's office when all this was promised to us. That's why I got mad when the contract came: It wasn't what they had promised us. The bond, the fee, the percentage, and the division—none of this was going to be done right. Even the area they had allowed me to apply for had been cut down. There was absolutely nothing there that they had promised me in order to get me to drop this litigation and sign a stipulation that I recognized the state boundary.

After Real Eight pulled out, what did you do?

I went into the marina business and started running dive trips from 1971 to 1972. During that time I kept trying to get the state to give me a division, but they kept making excuses. Finally, in 1972, I was approached by investors interested in forming another treasure hunting company. So we obtained the necessary contracts from the state and commenced work on the *San José* again. Right away we started hitting real good. We had not done that well when we left off, but it was that old magic of treasure hunting. You just get lucky sometimes.

What were you recovering?

Mostly gold, jewelry, and coins, but it was a real fluke. When I went back out there we first worked the main wreck site for a couple weeks and did very little. We found just a few items: a couple pillar dollars* and a few things like that.

But then we went out to where the *San José*'s rudder had been found, three hundred yards south of the main wreck site. We dug that whole area with the mailbox when Real Eight's big boat, the *Griffon*, was down. We dug craters out there three or four feet deep before we hit the hardpan and quit. But now I figured it wouldn't hurt to have a change of scenery, so we moved back out into that Sahara to do some more digging.

The first day I anchored up over the same spot where the rudder should have been, but it wasn't there. I learned later that

---

* Also called *Dos Mundos*, these round and rare silver coins were the first struck in Mexico in 1732 with the screw press.

another treasure hunter had stolen it, a two-ton twenty-five-foot rudder, and had shipped it up to Cincinnati, Ohio, where it stands in front of the Windjammer Restaurant.

Anyway we got out there and started digging in the same area. The only thing we found at the bottom of the hole was a big hawser, a rope about three inches thick.

I looked at that thing and it was going down into the hardpan. I said how could something that light be embedded in that hard, unbroken bottom? We had already made up our minds that nothing could have penetrated that bottom in a thousand years. That was why we stopped excavating the first time. But that rope got down there someway. I said, let's find out how.

I jammed up a blower and we blew about forty-five minutes and got a hole about eight inches deep into that hardpan. But the hawser was still there, still going into it. I did this about three times. Most of the divers just took off their equipment and laid around the deck and slept. We dug and dug and got about a foot and a half, and the damn hawser was still going down.

The next day we came back and started at it again. Finally, after about three feet of this hardpan, we broke through. Then it got real soft. It was like trenches down underneath this stuff. And, man, the things we began to find in there—swords, pistols, and rosaries . . .

How deep were you then below the substrate?

We were twelve to fifteen feet below the bottom of the hardpan. We had about three feet of hardpan, and then when we hit this soft stuff there was about five or six feet of that. Then these trenches. You could get down and sort of lay in them when you were picking up stuff. Once we started in it was just a matter of sitting there and hammering the hell out of it with the blower until we'd break it. Then we'd travel those trenches until they played out.

It appeared that when the ship came in she must have struck where the rudder came off, about three hundred yards from where she finally settled. And then the winds and her sunken condition, heeled her over onto her port side and she dragged across the bottom, gouging those trenches with her hull and rigging, dropping material off as she went along.

Underwater archaeologist Sonny Cockrell examines the remarkably well-preserved timbers of the San José, *which sank in 1733. The wood remains only because it was covered by protective sand until uncovered by salvage operations of the treasure hunters.*

Author Robert Burgess with a piece of ballast rock called egg ballast commonly found on Spanish shipwrecks. Since a different kind of rock ballast is found on English wrecks, this factor often aids in wreck identification. This particular wreck is the 243-year-old San José. (Courtesy W. A. Cockrell)

After we worked there awhile we determined this is what must have happened. We were recovering items that we had completely overlooked before, because they were buried twelve to fifteen feet deep.

We were really lucky. We went out not really expecting to do a lot. And then there we were getting coins; one good sized clump. But most were singles, pillar dollars, and some gold jewelry. We did real well.

Eventually, however, the artifacts began to peter out and so did our company's funds. They didn't want to put any more money into it and decided to shut down the operation. Several New York museums wanted the entire collection of artifacts that we had brought up and were willing to give us a sizeable write-off for taxes. The last thing I needed was a tax write-off. How the hell was I going to pay the crew?

At this point I knew I wasn't going to get anything out of it from the company. I hadn't gotten anything from the state since 1968, and this was 1973. I figured that if I was going to keep my crew and everything together I would have to actively pursue the division with the state for the 1968 stuff so I could at least pay the divers for the last two years work out of my portion from that.

So I went up to Tallahassee and really started pressuring Williams for a division. He said, "Oh, we'll be ready to divide with you in thirty or forty days." One thing led to another and he told me things that I had to do, like writing letters to the stockholders and everything, but it never seemed sufficient. There was always something else to do. Well, this went along through August when Bob Marx and I did some magnetometer work for the state. Then in September the state required me to go back to the old stockholders at Marine Tech, have a meeting with them, and explain what was happening with a defunct corporation and how it worked.

So on September 9, 1973, we had the meeting. Then I had to wait thirty days after that, the time that had to be given them to consider any objection to this thing, which put it into October. No objections came, so I wrote a letter to the state saying that we had had our meeting. I sent them copies and everything, and the next thing I got in November was a letter from the counsel for the secretary of state. It was a letter of transmittal by Williams and in the first paragraph it said, "We find your letter dated so and so is merely self-serving in your own behalf and not of any benefit, *et cetera, et cetera,* and since this was originally a court action of Monroe County, we feel that you should take this matter back to court."

Well, it didn't set too well with me. When this thing came up I went to my attorney and said, "What the hell do I do now?" He said, "Well, it looks like we're going to have to go to court." I said, "What does that mean?" He said, "About three months to get on the docket and be heard, and it's going to cost you maybe another five or six thousand dollars."

I said, "I don't have either one, time or money." He said, "Well, they've got you over a barrel again. You've got to do something."

At an archaeological laboratory in Tallahassee, a 410-pound "mystery box" recovered from a 1733 shipwreck off the Florida Keys is carefully raised out of its water bath prior to its opening by archaeologist Carl Clausen and assistants.

So, November went along, then December, and I was kinda mad at everybody by then. The company I was last with had already rooked me out of our last recoveries by deciding to donate the stuff, and the big problem was that the state had failed to pick up artifact material I had from 1972 and 1973. I still had it stored in barrels in my house and at the bank vault.

Back in August I had gone into the bank to take some stuff in that had come from the summer operations. I looked in the box and we had silver spoons and lockets and all types of things that just disintegrated. The bank bags that I had silver coins in had rotted and the bottom of the box was getting rusty. I figured they were going to charge me for the box if I wasn't careful, so I took all the stuff out and took some 409 and some sponges and tried to clean it up. I took the artifacts home and put them in water in an Igloo cooler chest about three feet from my bed, trying to preserve them, because I figured here was pretty valuable stuff just going to hell. It stayed there for two or three months.

Everything had gone so bad that in December I decided I had

Carl Clausen works over mystery chest recovered from the wreck of the San Fernando, *which sank in a hurricane in 1733.*

Significance of carved letters on end of chest remains a mystery. Center figures appear to read TBNE in combined letters. After the box was carefully opened by archaeologists, it was found to contain hundreds of sail-maker's awls, goods probably destined for the Spanish settlement at St. Augustine.

Jets of water must be constantly played over the chest to keep the wood from deteriorating.

to get away and think about things. I took my family to Georgia to visit my son. We were up there for the first two weeks in December, and during that time my other eighteen-year-old son who was staying home and going to college called and told me we got a notice that the doctor who owned the house that we were leasing had sold it. My lease was up on January first. He notified us that we had to leave the house. Here it was the middle of the season in the Keys and, man, you just don't find a place. So that compounded my problems.

Coming back from Georgia, I guess that must have been about the time that I formulated my plan. I just said, "To hell with the whole world. I've been burned every way I turn around and I'm not going to take it any more. I've had it up to my neck."

I knew I had to do something with the artifacts that I had, but I made up my mind that I wasn't going to turn them back over to the state of Florida. I haven't gotten anything from them for five years. The fifth anniversary was going to be December twenty-third. If I gave them this stuff and was ever lucky enough to get a division, I wasn't going to get anything because of the clowns at Undersea Mining.

So I said to hell with them, I think I'll just take the stuff back to the wreck site and let them go get the damn things themselves. Nobody had paid me to get them up. The state had not paid us and Undersea Mining had not paid us. Now I was not going to give them to them.

So I guess that was when I made my decision. It must have been about the middle of December. I said, "Come the fifth anniversary on December twenty-third, if they have not divided with me or shown some real good effort, that I'm going to dump this stuff right back on the wreck site."

And that's what I did. On the twenty-third of December they hadn't done anything. So I wrote a letter of resignation, sent copies to everyone I could—the governor, the secretary of state, Williams, Banberg of Undersea Mining—and told them I quit, that I was fed up, and that I didn't like the way they had been doing me—that I'm going to do something drastic.

On the twenty-fourth I started hauling this material out and back to the wreck site. I had a little old fourteen-foot boat with a twenty-horse motor. I made about three or four trips in the little boat, then the motor conked out. So I had a bunch of this stuff left.

I had a seventeen-foot Fiberglas boat in the yard. It had a big crack in the keel that we had tried to repair but couldn't. So I was stuck with this stuff on January first, when the weather finally got better. I launched the boat by myself, called this friend of mine, and said, "How about giving me a tow? I've got to move these artifacts around to another location."

He had no idea what I was going to do with them. I had called CBS the day before and said, "Look, there's something big going on." Jed Duval knew me well enough that, if I said it was, he knew to come down. So CBS was there early on the first.

When I got this friend of mine hooked up to the boat he towed me out through Tavernier Creek, and I told him to stop by the bridge where there were four guys from CBS. I said, "I can only take two of you." Jed Duval and John Smith, the cameraman, climbed aboard, then Gene Gate towed me out to the wreck site.

When we got there I told Gene I wanted to go on seaward about a thousand feet. I had one of those fifty-pound barbell flat weights tied to a nylon rope, and there was just enough scope to give me a good drag in the sea. So I tossed this over, then cut his tow loose, and as I drifted across those sand dunes, the Sahara desert out there, I started throwing that stuff out.

Were you throwing out anything valuable?

Absolutely. I started throwing stuff, and they circled around taking some shots. Then they came up to the stern of my boat and tied the bow of their boat off and we were having to fend off the boat—it was that close. I was standing in the stern. The cameraman was sitting right there about three feet away from my hands as I was picking up the stuff that I'd dumped out of the bank bags that I had put out there. I was holding it in front of the camera and then throwing it out. Jed Duval had the mike in front of my mouth saying, "And what is this?" and I would explain, gold rings and all this stuff, and then I threw them. Finally I just dumped the whole mess over right under the camera, but remember, I was drifting the whole time. And at the last, while I was busy doing everything, I looked down and I was knee-deep in water. The damn boat had leaked and . . . [laughing] I said, "To hell with it."

You were going down with the treasure?

Yeah. The boat just sank stern first. Boy, she went down in a hurry. I was out there wondering where in hell was that other boat. It was a long way to shore. But the seventeen-foot boat sank right on the wreck site. Of course, when I say wreck site that's a thousand foot radius, right?

That's right.

So it's within the confines of that wreck site. The state couldn't even find the seventeen-foot Fiberglas boat, much less an inch and a half diameter coin. That's why they said I didn't throw anything back—because they couldn't find it.

So this brought me up to where I am. They . . . I didn't expect them to react the way they did. You know I wanted to get some attention because I had written letters and made calls, and I couldn't get any satisfaction so I said to hell with it. I was going to do something that would draw some attention to this thing. Not only that, there was a number of inequities. The state had kept squeezing us over the last several years by their contracts that were getting tighter and tighter to where now their contracts are unworkable, you know, not on the basis that *we* have to work with. It was just a matter of time before somebody did something. I guess I was the one that was up to bat.

What about the coins that were allegedly salvaged within the last couple years off the San José *that turned up recently for auction on the West Coast?*

Well, that's peculiar. You know, people get the idea that, I guess, being a treasure hunter and under state contract that I can't own coins. On the contrary, I have the right to own coins, probably more than anybody else because I have been gathering them since 1964. Those coins were coins from a private collection that my wife has. She scrounged those things from me over the years, and some of them were even possibly off the *San José* that had gone through two different processes back before the state's action. But they were absolutely not part of the 1972 or 1973 salvage. The coins that were in those auctions were coins that we had.

After everything blew up, the only way to raise money was to sell some of this stuff that we had from back then.

What are they charging you with?

I don't know right now. The way I understand it is grand larceny.

Tom, if this thing ever gets straightened out, do you antici-pate getting back into treasure hunting business again?

Well, there would have to be an awful lot of changes. Right now the only thing I would consider would have to be out of the country. With the state and the conditions as they exist, I couldn't work—even if I didn't have this. I have no plans at the moment, but things could change tomorrow. I would like to go back and work the *San José* and get the stuff I threw back.

I hope somebody does.

Well, I'll have to say this, some of the material wasn't just inadvertently thrown, some of it was placed very gingerly to the winds, some of it was placed very gingerly to the point that I could go back . . . I know exactly where it is. Like I tell a lot of people, "The bottom of the ocean is my ball park, and I know it like the back of my hand." I know where to go, so I may get back on the *San José* one day.

6 ~~~~

John Baker: Statues in a Spring

Twenty-seven-year-old John Baker is of average height, with a lean, muscular build, dark hair, intense blue eyes, and a trim Fu Manchu mustache. He dresses casually, is soft-spoken and unassuming. Baker seldom volunteers information or elaborates on answers unless pressed for details—possibly a trait of his profession.

We interviewed him at his home near Bristol, Florida, in a livingroom surrounded by a variety of North and Central American artifacts: plaques of mounted projectile points; carved-stone temple furniture; a bear skull inlaid with semiprecious green stones; boxes of complete or fragmentary polychrome effigies and pottery; a glass-covered tray of small ceramic pieces, including several gold-washed copper pendants; carved jade amulets; and crescent-shaped flint nose rings. The treasure hunter had just returned from an artifact gathering expedition to Costa Rica. Two 800-pound stone statues brought back with him were still tied down on a flatbed trailer behind his house.

John, how did you happen to get into this business?

I've always been interested in treasure hunting as a hobby, and one day I decided to go into it full time.

What were you doing with it as a hobby?

I was diving on weekends, diving all the sinks and rivers and searching for something to find in this area and in south Florida.

And you were finding what type of artifacts?

Polychrome bowls, regular ceramic bowls, mastodon teeth, fossil shark teeth, arrowheads—all the common material found here in the southeastern United States.

Were many of these items from burial sites? Or how did they come to be there?

Many came from burial sites. Many came from living sites that were eventually covered by water. In the Wakulla River I did a couple that were evidently a living site, and either the water changed paths or just washed into it and brought a lot of bone needles out of there with inlay work, *et cetera.* You could find charcoal in the water there with the pots, all mixed together.

Were you finding the fragments of the pots?

Right.

Were you hand-fanning everything at that time?

Yes. Just doing it strictly as an amateur.

How did you get your leads to know where to look?

When I first started doing it, I just went blindly chasing off; then I eventually learned to look at charts and maps. If you can read a chart you can about tell where any Indians were camped and then you can find it in a few minutes.

What would you look for on the map?

Points on rivers or lakes, high elevations, water, three or four lakes together with elevations between, rock outcroppings. Where you found exposed rock close to the ground, that was used for their working places, where the Indians picked up flint to make arrowheads. They generally picked up their flint and carried it many miles before they made the arrowheads. They very seldom made them where they picked up the flint.

What maps were you using?

Quad sheets, quadrangle maps. You can take one of these for a certain locale and pinpoint areas that you want to check out. Or better yet, you can go into the library and take overlays of area maps and run them all the way back to get different types of information. For example, maps of a couple hundred years ago will show recent Indian sites.

Where do these maps come from?

Here in northwest Florida it is the Department of Archives. Most states have the same set-up. I found the maps on file at Florida State University. So this is probably true in other state and university libraries.

That's interesting. If you find the map showing the Indian site, then that's where you look?

Right. And if the map shows an Indian site two hundred years ago, chances are good that it may have been a living site five thousand years ago, if it's the right area. In many fields in Leon County [Tallahassee area], I picked up points that would run anywhere from the Paleo Period [14,000 to 10,000 B.P.*] on up to 800 B.C.

How old were you when you were doing this?

When I was in grade school, I was collecting arrowheads as a hobby. I just followed it on into my teens and older, then went into it full time.

When did you start diving for artifacts?

Well, I skindived when I was very young, since I lived right in front of a lake. Then I started scuba diving when I went into the service in 1964. I've been diving for about twelve years.

In pursuing this hobby, I imagine you were looking for old bottles, too, weren't you?

Right. I used to do a lot of bottle hunting, but I've mostly gotten out of that now. I used to get a lot of black glass and the usual run of the mill bottles.

Were you selling these items at the time?

A few of them, not many. I'd keep a good piece if I found it. I didn't really know how to market a piece back then. I didn't know

* Before present time.

who to talk to. That has a lot to do with it. You can sell something that is worth a fortune for nothing if you don't know what you are doing.

How did you finally learn what the value was of these pieces, since they often are unique?

They don't have any specific sheet like a stock market report or something that gives the current prices of those things. You have to more or less live with them, see other people sell them, go to the places that handle them until you eventually acquire a price range. There is no set price on an item like this. They don't make them anymore, so you can't put a price on them. You can charge five dollars for a bottle somebody else has dug, or a dollar for it. There is no way you can reproduce that bottle. Once you sell it for a dollar you are not going to get another one. So you might as well put a price on it that is worthwhile, because if they went out to dig that bottle it probably would cost them thirty dollars by the time they got themselves into the woods or wherever they were going to get it.

What branch of the service were you in?

Army special forces. I did quite a bit of underwater work at a training school in Hawaii, then spent eighteen months in Viet Nam.

When you came back from there, what did you do?

Went to college for a while majoring in architectural design, then I eventually went into oceanography. And then I quit and went to work for Disney World for a while; then I came back to Tallahassee and went in with a partner selling artifacts, doing this part-time. I supplied him with the bottles and things he sold. I was also going to school part-time and driving trucks at night. Then I went to work for a Tallahassee dive shop and finally quit and went into the artifact business full time for myself.

Could you tell me about the effigy you found while you worked at the dive shop?

Well, a friend of mine and I from Tallahassee decided to check out a couple of leads I had on some Indian mounds in Mississippi. So we packed up and headed out there to Ocean Springs and dived a couple of mounds on the bay. There is a spring in the area and, as we dived down to it, I saw just the top of the head of the figure sticking out. We were in thirty-five or forty feet of water, no more than twenty or thirty feet back in the cave, just under the lip of it.

Well, when I saw it I pulled on the head, expecting it to come out, but it didn't. I pulled out my knife and had to dig it out of the sand and pulled out the entire effigy, except for a few little chips. We got a couple decent black glass bottles out of there, and there is a lot of ballast stone in there. It was a docking place for early ships with old pilings sticking up not far down from the spring. We figured they probably stopped in there to replenish their fresh water or to wash their sails. Although the piece looked like some of the finer polychrome pottery that comes from Mississippi, we figured it had to have been on a boat or something, picked up in trade, and it was dropped overboard.

Could you give me the dimensions?

It was about eight inches high, three inches at the bottom, and the pipe hole at the back was an inch and a quarter. It had red arm bands on both arms, with a headdress. Small hole in the mouth, evidently for incense or something like that.

Why do you suppose it was not found before?

At that particular time there was not much activity in Mississippi. It is one of the few states that does not have an archives system. They do not pursue their archaeological past too much out there. Very few people even dive out there. Not that many are into it, unless it is commercial diving. The water visibility is often very bad. This was just one of these places that had unusually good visibility.

How did you go about it when you went into the business full time?

First I was setting up consignments in shops, selling at flea markets or through ads in the paper. People would call or write me. Then I started doing nationwide shows. They run them in the malls throughout the United States.

Could you explain how a show is set up?

Take a typical town like Cincinnati, Ohio, for instance. You go into a mall there and set up and it is promoted as an artifact

show or a gem and mineral show. Dealers will be there with different types of material. One man will have fantastic crystal specimens, while another will have geode specimens. And I always had
artifacts. You set up, say, on a Thursday and stay until Saturday.
You hit a lot of the local trade, but you are also going to pick up
people who are interested in just these items. They have been
doing these shows for five or six years and they have gained a lot of
publicity. People look for them. Also you make contacts that in-
variably lead to new contacts.

*Did these things that you sold at the shows finance your fur-
ther searches?*

Yes, along with other things, they did. When you first start off
you sell the things you have, then you get to the point where you
just don't have time to go hunting anymore. Now I have reached
the point where I buy a lot of things, collections that people want
to sell. I'll break it down and resell it.

*What was the first trip you made to find items where you
were more than just a state away from your home base?*

About a year and a half ago we went into Central America;

*Treasure hunter John
Baker with an ancient cer-
emonial vase he recovered
on one of his expeditions
to Central America.*

Mexico. It was strange the first time going off like that. It was some adventure.

Tell me about it.

Well, I had met this friend of mine who had been going into the country for many years. And I would advise anyone that wanted to do this to go with someone who has already been going into the country and doing this. If you go in blind, you will really get into trouble or run into a lot of problems that are unbelievable. So I went with this fellow and we flew into San José, Costa Rica, and met his wife and stayed there a few days. Then she carried us out into the surrounding area of the mountains. You'd be driving along and beside the road there would be pots and things sticking out of the side of the cliff or where the road bed cut through. Nobody bothered with them. Small clay effigy heads, they were actually building roads on them.

When you saw this, did you stop and hunt or did you go to specific localities?

We stopped when we saw something. But we had a couple specific areas there that we worked. We did a lot of shoveling and water work.

What was the water work?

It would be a well or sink, something usually about eighty feet in diameter. The deepest one I was in ran about sixty or seventy feet deep—mostly limestone with heavy silt bottom.

And were you just looking for items rather than using any type of air lift or dredge?

We would find part of a complex that had caved in. We were more interested in doing that type. We weren't actually going down and dredging. We would have to find a really good land site before we would go into the water to look any further.

Tell me about your largest find there.

Well, we found two stone figures that weigh eight hundred pounds apiece. We had worked this temple complex for two days and were digging up a lot of nice things. Part of the complex had caved into this cenote or sink. I went down to see what might turn up on the bottom, and I spotted these two stone figures lying side-by-side. Evidently they had fallen in from above. It took us two days of hard work to get them up with fifty-five-gallon drums used as lifts. Got a bunch of laborers there to help us pull them out and get them into San José. Then we flew them out. It cost us seven hundred dollars air freight to get the two of them back to the United States. They are some kind of local volcanic-like rock. We haven't established how old they are yet.

Now how are you covering your expenses on these trips?

Just from what I make as a silver craftsman and from the artifacts and items I sell. If I don't sell anything, I don't eat that week.

Have you found it a profitable business?

It can be, but you have to work for it. It's not an easy business. You have to really put everything you have into it. Primarily I do it because I like the adventure involved. But it seems you can't have the one without the other.

Have you found any gold items?

Yes. In Costa Rica we found a few rain frogs. These are nice; their design looks almost ultra-modern. Their feet are long and flat and there is a little decorative work on the upper side. You find very few that are solid gold. Most are gold-washed copper. A lot of trade bead type material for necklaces, stone beads, small Venetian glass beads. These latter are relatively young items, only four or five hundred years old. Whereas the rain frogs and other pieces go way back.

Could you tell us something about the problems an individual might have who would be interested in doing this kind of treasure hunting?

There are so many problems you could do a whole story on just them. The major difficulties are finding the stuff, getting it out, finding a market, knowing how to catalog the artifacts after you do get them, how to sell them, what to keep and what to sell.

Do you have problems of dealing with government officials down there?

We didn't have, but I understand that things have changed in Costa Rica and they are not letting people take out what they used to be able to. Mexico is real rough. I would not recommend even trying to bring a reproduction out of Mexico. They will definitely give you trouble if you try to take out their artifacts, and you may have a lot of trouble proving an item is simply a reproduction.

Could you give me an idea what your expenses would be on an expedition like that?

Well, just your living expenses for a month will run about fifteen hundred dollars. Your shipping expenses to get the things back to the states is where you run into money. It is based on the weight of the items, for example the seven hundred dollars on our statues. And you may have to hold these items a year or more before you sell them. And then you may never sell them. Sometimes it's worse to bring a piece out like that. Definitely, if I were going to do it, I would use air freight instead of ship lines, because with ship lines you have many problems with the law, customs, broken items, and things like that—like a friend of mine just shipped fifteen hundred pounds of items and the ship lines went broke. He hasn't found his shipment yet, and he had already paid for the expense of them being shipped. With air freight you don't have that problem.

Have you had any problems with people trying to rip you off down there?

I haven't, but I've had friends who have been.

Do you carry any protection or anything?

No, you can't. You can acquire firearms in a country, but you can't bring them in. So we don't have any guns with us.

How are you staying in the field—do you camp or what?

You're usually not far from a town somewhere, so we stay at the local hotels and hire the inexpensive transportation there to get us to where we want to go. Generally you don't have to spend a lot of money in these countries if you are careful. It is a lot cheaper than the United States.

Do you speak Spanish?

Very little. Just a few words. The people I go with do. My friend's wife speaks several dialects. My friends and I usually make an annual trip for a couple of weeks.

How large would you say an average shipment of artifacts would be?

Three, four hundred pots at a time. Maybe a couple hundred pounds of celts. Your golden pieces and things like that you cannot legally bring out. But once in a while some of them do arrive in the States. In just general figures, maybe a couple hundred pounds, but on the average you don't bring that much out at a time unless you really find something large because of the air freight. When we speak of three hundred or four hundred pots, they would range in size from four to five inches in diameter to two to three feet. They take a lot of space because of the way they have to be packed.

Do you do all your packing?

Yes, it is quite a job in itself. Generally we buy trunks and ship them inside, or buy plywood and build boxes.

Are those whole pots, or pieces?

Both. We bring out broken ones if they have particularly nice designs and good paint. It is worth bringing them out. It does not matter that much. In fact, for some reason, sometimes a pot sells better if it is broken and then pieced together.

What criteria do you use in selecting pieces you bring back—their uniqueness, perhaps?

Yes, I definitely look for one-of-a-kind pieces. Or something with highly decorated work to it—something that makes it really unique, something that you seldom see—maybe a color. They have many different colors to their polychrome work, and some of them are quite rare. A blue and a black color made out of fish blood, for example. Anything with that, even fragments are valuable.

What is polychrome?

A two color item, usually a red and a darker red. Most all the pottery found here in northwest Florida is your shell temper. Then you start getting into your Mississippi and Upper Mississippi Valley and you run into a lot of things that are a polychrome that is very similar to pre-Columbian work. It has more workmanship to it. It has been fired harder, and it has colors on it, where the shell temper does not. Shell temper may be one color or brown, depending upon whichever area where they were processing the clay.

Do you carry your diving gear with you on these trips?

Yes, we'll carry our regulators, wet suits, things like that.

Do you have any problem about finding air?

Out in the boonies you would, but the larger ports have a setup for Americans coming in to dive the shoreline, and there are not many problems getting air in these areas.

Do you work a hookah* at all?

I don't like it, because I'd get tangled up in trees and other underwater debris where I work. Even in shallow water I'd rather wear a tank. The air hose bothers me back there.

Have you run into any venomous snakes in the water?

Not often. Once in a while you encounter cottonmouth moccasins in Florida, and in Costa Rica they have a couple of vipers that are pretty bad. But I've never had too many problems with snakes.

Could you give me an idea of the price range on the items you sell?

Some artifacts go for as low as a dollar; others I have sold for as high as eight thousand dollars apiece. The latter would be your pre-Columbian art. I have sold a few collections of American Indian items for large sums of money.

What has been your single most valuable piece?

That would be hard to say. I don't really place a value on a single piece. You see a lot of nice pieces and eventually you get to the point where it becomes an everyday thing—where someone else might ah and ooh about them.

I mean priced as valuable. Have you sold any single item for several thousand?

I've sold a stone piece for fifteen hundred dollars. That was a stone metate. It was Mayan from Costa Rica.

Are the people that buy your pieces also collectors or in the business?

Many are in the business, a lot are private collectors, and many are people buying decorative pieces to go in their homes.

Have any museums bought from you?

A few pieces were sold to the Smithsonian. Others have been on display at the Tallahassee Junior Museum. A few at the

---

* A diving unit that employs a hose to supply a diver with air from a surface compressor.

Columbus College museum in Columbus, Georgia. Their professor of art there has bought quite a few pieces.

What plans are you making for future expeditions?

We're trying to set up a unique service that will combine
diving, digging, and touring. We're talking about a fifteen-day
trip totaling fifteen-hundred dollars for a round trip with everything furnished. This will include transportation from our depar-
ture point in Florida to whatever area we are working in Yucatan
or Costa Rica. We will carry them into the sites and let them
actually dig on some. We cannot guarantee what they will be able
to bring out, but we will take them to unusual places that few
people have an opportunity to see—a once-in-a-lifetime trip. There
will be qualified divers along, and those who wish can participate
in this. There are many unexplored wrecks in Central and South
America that are just waiting to be looked over. In other areas
they will be digging for black glass on some of the banana planta-
tions down there.

When do you anticipate this program to be operational?

Hopefully as soon as possible, perhaps sometime in 1976.

*Has your treasure hunting for historical artifacts ever been
criticized from the standpoint of disturbing cultural items that
may be of later significance to archaeological studies of the area?*

No, on the contrary. I feel that everyone should try to preserve and appreciate things of the past. This is not just a game to
make money. If it were not for people like me, most of these pieces
would be lost or destroyed. By bringing them back and making
them available for people to enjoy again, I feel that these artifacts
are once again serving a useful purpose.

*Other than the money, what do you personally get out of this
kind of treasure hunting?*

Well, it's what I want to do. It's my life. It's a lot of back-
aches, hard work, and little sleep, but it gives me all the pleasure I
could hope for. And someday it will fulfill all the dreams I have
for it.

The search is definitely thrilling. It's like the first time out
the door with a parachute. It's something you have to experience
to appreciate. Even if you've done it a hundred times, there is
something there when you jump out.

7 ~~~~

Robert F. Marx: My Phantom Wreck

I first met Bob Marx at an underwater paleontology and archaeology seminar at Daytona Beach, Florida. He is a tall, blue-eyed, amiable fellow with unruly sandy hair and mustache, who seems already to have crowded a lifetime of adventures into his thirty-nine years.

Starting with his search for the Civil War *Monitor* off Cape Hatteras in 1955, Marx went on to explore cenotes in Yucatan, dive up hundreds of artifacts from a 1741 shipwreck off Quintana Roo, Mexico, excavate the sunken city of Port Royal for the Jamaican government, recover treasure from Spanish shipwrecks off Florida and the Bahamas, and participate in underwater archaeological expeditions in the Mediterranean. In addition, he sailed as captain aboard a replica of Columbus's smallest ship, the *Niña*, duplicating that historical voyage across the Atlantic; nearly accomplished the same feat in a Viking ship, and somehow also found time to write of his many adventures in hundreds of magazine articles and fifteen books.

Unlike many divers lured into the search for sunken treasure, Marx's knowledge of underwater archaeology and his tenacious love for ferreting out facts from the archives has enabled him not only to follow the clues to the wrecks, but to go beyond them into the fascinating history of their past.

In the monologue that follows, Marx describes his long quest for the treasure ship *Maravilla,* an inordinately rich wreck for which he had been searching so long without success that his friends called it Marx's phantom wreck. The material reflects, I believe, the typical Marx enthusiasm for his subject. It also says something about the inner drive of the man—the same drive reflected to a greater or lesser degree in all such hunters, whether they search for adventure, treasure, or simply historical knowledge.

I was looking for the wreck of the *Maravilla* every year from 1960 on. Each year I would spend one or two months in the Bahamas trying to find it. I first became interested in the wreck when I went to Spain in 1959 and dug up some documents at the Spanish archives. I spent three years in the archives at Seville doing research on thousands of shipwrecks. Ever since that time I have maintained one to three people doing research for me, depending upon how rich I am at the time. My wife and I make one or two trips a year there to keep ourselves up-to-date on what's happening.

I got interested in the *Maravilla* when I found a book published in 1657 by a clergyman who was one of the fifty-five survivors of the seven hundred people that were on the ship when she wrecked. He wrote a complete book about his experiences, and it was fascinating. He told every detail from the time he left Lima, Peru, until he was shipwrecked. He talked about the priests charging two hundred pesos to hear confessions, and when the ship broke up they were the first to drown because their pockets were filled with gold.

I also found twelve thousand pages of documents in Spain, in the Vatican, in England, and in several other places, all on this wreck. There was so much documentation on the *Maravilla* because it was the second richest wreck ever lost in the western hemisphere. (The richest is a ship that was lost off Cartagena, Colombia, in two thousand feet of water. I don't think anybody is going to find it in the near future.) The *Maravilla* was carrying five and a half million pieces of eight—two hundred and sixty tons of silver. I found three maps pinpointing the site. And I probably found it ten years before I knew it. I didn't read all of those twelve thousand pages of documents, unfortunately.

I started looking for this wreck thinking that there were fifty-eight iron cannons aboard it. So in doing magnetometer surveys I was expecting a real big anomaly.* I probably went over it many, many times because I actually searched a hundred and fifty square miles of that bank. In the course of searching for it, we found seventy-six wrecks, several hundred anchors, and two Pershing missile cones.

We knew the wreck was in fifty feet of water, but we still had to search the shallow places. The *Maravilla* was on its way home with twenty-two other ships when it collided with one and got a big hole in it. Since the seas were rough, the captain decided to run it aground. He hit a reef and then the ship slipped off into deeper water. So we also had to search these shallow reefs for clues. It turned out to be exactly where the documents said it was: in twenty-seven degrees fifteen minutes of latitude.

My mistake was that I had not read all of these documents years ago. If I had, I would have learned that the *Maravilla* carried all bronze cannon, and a magnetometer does not give a reading for bronze.

On one of the maps I used, it said "The Plate Wreck." That's my wreck. Sir William Phips, who later salvaged a wreck on Silver Shoals in 1683, went to the *Maravilla* in 1680 and brought up a couple buckets of coins. He made the chart showing the Plate Wreck, which means silver and gold.

Our salvage vessel was the *Griffon.* I first used it when I

* A deviation in the earth's magnetic field caused by a concentration of iron.

worked for Real Eight on the east coast of Florida. We have a split sleeping place for fourteen people. A blaster is mounted on the stern. It has several types of navigating equipment, a radar, three different types of radios, and a cruising range of over twenty thousand miles.

In 1972 I joined forces with Willard Bascomb, the famous oceanographer. We formed a company called Sea Finders, raised some money from some Wall Street backers, bought the *Griffon* from Real Eight, and formed our own company. We spent four months out there, from April through July. By August we were almost bankrupt and ready to head to Cartagena for another wreck down there.

During the summer we searched several different ways. In previous years my wife and I spent three months doing a visual survey over the whole bank, locating several wrecks from the air. One was an 1860 three-hundred-and-thirty-foot-long steel-hull sailing ship that was lost in a hurricane. By then salvaging was such a flourishing profession that they stripped these things bare.

Dick Anderson, my partner now on the wreck, found one of those brass hatch covers. I kept saying, "Man, it's worthless, forget about it." He was bringing them up and I was throwing them overboard. When I got out to California, I went into some of these chandler's shops and saw the same hatch covers. They sell them for three hundred dollars each. In one night I had thrown about thirty of them away.

A lot of these wrecks we could find either from a plane or just dragging a diver behind the boat on what we called the Shark Line. We called it that because, when you looked back, you either saw a gobbler or a couple barracuda following you.

With the magnetometer, if we passed within a quarter of a mile of a mass such as a pile of anchor chain, we would probably get an anomaly. We were using the same type of magnetometer that was invented by Fay Fields, who used to work for Mel Fisher's Treasure Salvors and then Real Eight.

Eventually I realized my mistake—that I was not looking for sixty-eight iron cannon, I was looking for bronze cannon. So I could only hope that there were enough anchors on the wreck to

give me a good anomaly. A lot of times when these ships were lost they threw their anchors overboard before they wrecked, so we were not sure what we would find. Normally we made passes spaced out about two to three hundred feet, because we could pick up an iron cannon or a big anchor with this type of proton magnetometer at about two hundred feet. But because I was looking really for a needle in a haystack, I knew I might have to find this wreck by locating just a small pile of cannonballs or ship's fittings. Since we had to make our runs fifty feet apart, in that three to four month period in 1972, we covered thirty-five square miles making fifty-foot lanes.

Sometimes when we found an anomaly, we checked it out by putting on a mask and sticking our heads over the side. If we saw it was a modern anchor, we kept going. About fifty percent of the anomalies were buried under sand, so every three or four days we would stop the magnetometer work and use the blaster or prop wash to dig on them. Usually it would take one hole, and I could determine whether or not it was the wreck I was after, the *Mara-villa*.

On three occasions we punched a hole and found gold and silver coins, and I almost had a mutiny each time saying, "Okay, if it's the wrong period and the wrong wreck, let's go," because the crew got a share of what was found and they weren't happy about leaving a wreck with gold and silver on it to go and look for a wreck that they called my phantom wreck. Nobody believed it existed because everybody, from Ed Link on down the line, had looked for it for the last twenty years, but nobody had ever found it. In fact people wrote articles before I found it, saying, "Marx invented the wreck. It never existed to begin with." So that was part of the reason I was trying to find it.

Our blaster was very strong. Normally we would have one or two divers off to the side, and we had a mercury switch where they could signal the surface to slow it down. Sometimes we would dig down to a chain, which meant it was after 1830. The type of wooden stock would tell us perhaps that it was before 1840, maybe 1830. So even though we might cover a large area the size of a football field, finding that, I would know that it was the wrong wreck. So we would start magging again. This went on fourteen to sixteen hours a day, from the minute we had any daylight. While one boat was dragging the magnetometer, another boat was laying out a series of buoys. In some cases we would use two magnetometers.

The way we finally found the wreck was a fluke. The first day of the year, I had started exactly where the Spaniards had said and where I had started many other times. Right near there was a modern wreck, and in this spot we would get a tiny anomaly. Every day I used to go over this spot to test the magnetometer. And as I said, after searching thirty-five square miles around that spot at fifty-foot lanes both with magnetometers and visually and not finding it, I finally said let's go back to that spot. A storm came up. We had a little dispute on board, so we pulled the anchor up and two ballast stones were snagged onto the flukes of the anchor. We had been on it all year, anchoring over it. I had not realized it because we thought that small anomaly was the nearby modern wreck. In fact, mixed in with the wreck of the *Maravilla*, we found many parts of that modern wreck, so we got tricked.

We blasted the first hole. Only one of the fellows I had aboard was a diver; most of the others were oceanographic students. The first coin I uncovered I cleaned underwater, and there it was, 1655, so I was pretty sure that it was the *Maravilla*. By then we had been out for several weeks and were out of food, so we supplemented the rice and beans we had left by catching lobsters and shooting a few fish.

The visibility over there is usually about two hundred feet, so it is fantastic. But when you are blasting, you are stirring up the water. The first thing we found was the bow section, so we started working there. The depth of the water where the goodies were was about fifty feet. But most of the water depth was twenty-five feet. We had to blow away twenty-five feet of sand to reach the wreck. The best wrecks, like the *Maravilla*, are usually deeply buried under sand or mud or ten feet of coral.

The bronze cannon we found were all ten and a half to eleven and a half feet long, weighing one and a half to two and a half tons, depending upon the width.

An interesting thing about the ballast: About half of it turned out to be silver ore about ninety-five percent pure. We had been throwing this away for weeks until I finally took some to FIT* and had it analyzed. About ten percent of it was ballast rock that came from Tuscany, Italy—from the same mines where Michelangelo and different Italian sculptors made beautiful works of art. It would have been interesting if we had dug just one hole and had the ballast analyzed, found it was Italian rock from Tuscany, and said, "Well, it can't be a Spanish wreck because it has got Italian ballast." That's the kind of thing you have to be careful about.

None of the film footage I made of the recovery was fake. When I had cameras down there I shot. Sometimes we were so busy picking up goodies, mapping, and recording and everything that I missed a lot of good stuff. We found many clumps of silver coins in the shape of the original bag. Sometimes the bag was crushed, so that you could see that the bags were flattened out. On

* Florida Institute of Technology in Melbourne, Florida.

our second day we found six hundred pounds of silver coin clumps, which is about sixty-five thousand or eighty thousand pieces of eight.

Interestingly, we rarely saw anyone out there. We were in the Bermuda Triangle, but I don't believe much in that. The few times we did see anyone out there, they were pirates coming out to pirate our goodies from us. It was totally out of the shipping lanes.

Other than a small part of the bow section, we found very few pieces of wood. Almost all of it was deteriorated. We found a few pieces of wooden furniture made of teak. Until now we've found only five intact olive jars, but we uncovered four thousand necks. There were at least four thousand of them in the bow section alone. They carried water, wine, vinegar, olive oil, gunpowder— just about anything. They are much like the amphoras carried on Greek and Roman wrecks abroad.

After the *Maravilla* hit the reef, it slid off, still intact. About three or four hours later, with all these people on there waiting to be rescued, a norther started. You can imagine the chaos. Hundreds perished and only a relatively few survived.

We filmed the recovery of the first silver bar that we found just as it happened. As I said there was two hundred and sixty tons of these silver ingots on there. Most of them weighed seventy or eighty pounds. We also found one that weighed two hundred and fifty-five pounds and one a hundred and sixty pounds. Some of them were also very small.

We had a youngster with us who had never dived before. At the last minute before leaving Fort Pierce I said, "How about working for us?" He was only seventeen years old. The first time he started picking up silver ingots he was so excited that he put three of the bars in the basket, which made it weigh two hundred and forty pounds. I went underneath the thing, trying to help it up. When the basket got to the surface, the line broke and eighty-pound silver bars came raining down around my head. In a period of five days, the youngster was involved with picking up a million or two million dollars worth of treasure, so he was pretty excited when he got home. Then he had to go back to high school.

Willard Bascomb, my partner, was not really much of a diver. But at that time we were so busy that every time we punched a hole to bring the stuff up, Willard became a diver in a big hurry. A couple other people we had working with us turned out to be pirates working for rival treasure hunting groups—spying, not really diving. We had a captain from Daytona. The minute he hit shore he called up everybody in the treasure hunting business and offered the location of the *Maravilla* for twenty-five hundred dollars. We had to set the fear of God in his heart. Then he disappeared, taking a couple sacks of coins with him.

Unlike many wrecks we worked, where you have only a few feet of sand and as you are digging you are blowing it away to expose a large section of the wreck, this one was different. Every time we blew a hole in the bottom about sixty feet in diameter, we found all the goodies right on the hardpan. We would stop the blaster to let the water clear up, then I would make my mosaic, take all my pictures of the artifacts, then we would start picking them up. When we moved sixty or eighty feet away for the next hole, the sand out of that hole filled the previous one, so that we never saw more than a sixty-foot diameter at any one time. And overnight, the last hole of the day would be totally covered by the next morning, because there is a two- to three-knot current on that bank.

The silver bars look like loaves of bread. Half the treasure on the *Maravilla* came from South America, and the other half from Mexico. Usually that was not the case, but this is what happened: The fleet was coming back with the treasures of South America when they learned of an English fleet waiting off Havana to intercept them. So the Spanish sailed over to Vera Cruz and picked up all the treasures of Mexico. That is why the *Maravilla* was the second richest ship. It was not only carrying three years of treasure rather than the usual one-year amount from South America; it also got a three-year supply from Mexico.

In the morning the weather was always calm; by afternoon it was pouring rain and squalls. Everyone thinks it's real romantic, but it is really hard work when you are working on a wreck. A lot of people would not dig doing that in fifty feet of water ten and twelve hours a day. But when you are picking up treasure you can't worry about it. The bends and decompression will tell you.

But that's what it is, hard work. All the ballast was moved by hand, but luckily the *Maravilla* had so much treasure there was not much rock ballast.

The gold coins were interesting, because even though they started minting silver coins in the 1540s in the New World, the first gold coins were minted in the 1630s, and the first ones that were ever carried back from South America—or anyplace in the New World—were on the *Maravilla*. So the oldest gold coins minted in the New World were lost on the *Maravilla*. They are smaller than a piece of eight. There are actually two escudos to one fourth of an ounce.

The loose silver coins are about three times normal thickness, heavily sulphided and much harder to clean. The big clumps of coins were easy because you just tapped on them and they fell to pieces. The coins inside were as shiny as the day they were made.

The gold coins were minted in Bogota, Colombia. The silver came from Mexico City; Lima, Peru; and Potosí, Peru (the last is in Bolivia today). The silver consisted of one-ounce pieces of eight along with half-ounce pieces of four, two, and one.

The first silver bar was covered with coral growth, which proves that at one time the wreck was uncovered—otherwise coral could not have grown on it. Six months after the Spaniards lost the wreck, they came back to salvage it. Finding only a few pieces of wreckage, they salvaged about five percent of the treasure and then said that the thing was totally covered over. For the next thirty to forty years they went back to the same location, but it was always covered over.

After notifying the Bahamians that we had found this wreck, rather than try to go all the way to Nassau, which was about two hundred and fifty miles from the wreck, we came into Fort Pierce and deposited the treasure in eleven different banks. We tried to spread it around so that there would not be a lot of gold fever and people following us.

But it didn't work. As soon as we got back to the wreck we had planes circling us, and almost every day we had boats out there. One couple came out actually with bazookas. That's not joking either. I didn't know it at the time, but one of my deck crew had notified all of his treasure hunting friends, and when we got out there a mob of boats followed.

Even though all my coins were dated right, I checked everything against the original manifest. The Spanish always made three copies. The flagship would carry one, the ship that was carrying the goodies would carry one, and one would be left in the home port until word came back that the fleet was safe.

I cleaned one of the silver bars and could see the ANA—for Antonio Navada—so I matched up these marks with those on the manifest, the tally mark, the weight mark, the seals that the church's tenth had been paid, that the king's twentieth had been paid. Then I knew positively that we had found the right wreck.

Of course when we took all this material into a bank and people saw those encrusted bars that looked like loaves of bread, they were curious about what they were. We told them they were moon rocks.

My partner, Willard Bascomb, was the man who started Operation Mohole about fifteen years ago, drilling a hole through the crust of the earth. He designed the *Alcoa Sea Probe*, which we later used on several occasions for deep water treasure. In fact, we formed Sea Finders originally to go after deepwater wrecks using the *Sea Probe*. But it did not work. We were trying to work in three to five thousand feet of water, and the currents were too great. So we went after the *Maravilla*, or Marx's phantom wreck, as it was known in those days. Nobody believed that it existed.

I had learned that after they wrecked, this norther started up with winds sixty to seventy knots. The ship broke in three pieces and the treasure was scattered over a large area. So far we had only worked on the bow section, and I am the only one who knows where the rest of the wreck is.

The first time we came in and deposited all those goodies, I had to find a new crew. I left Bascomb ashore to handle all the business with the Bahamians, and I ended up with a total of eight divers besides myself. Charlie, the captain, was from New Smyrna Beach. He is really tough. When I found him, his jaw was swollen out about three inches. He had been out fishing on his own boat alone, got a toothache, pulled out a tooth with his pliers, didn't get the right one, pulled out another . . . pulled out four teeth before he finally got the right one. So this is the kind of guy I needed on the boat.

We went out there, the squalls came, and then the first plane. It circled around us to get the radio bearing with some station on the mainland, and then it went away. The next day the boats were out there. We'd either jump in the small skiff and run out with the machine gun and chase them away, or they'd come alongside and we'd wave them off. In most cases they'd go away without us having to threaten them.

We had this one diver from Panama in the crew. We kept saying to this guy, "Worse diver we ever had." He never found anything. After he left he bought a marina and a whole bunch of other things with emeralds and gold coins he stole from us. He turned out to be one of the best divers, but we just didn't realize it.

Once the blaster got working, we'd get down to bedrock, and you just barely had it fanning so it took small grains of sand away at a time. While that was going on, you had to move all the ballast, too. And on the hardpan were all these little pockets about the size of your palm that small things like emeralds, diamonds, and rubies got caught in. So you fanned those out. Then we got back to the same old deal, bringing up silver bars again. A couple times I found out that the guys were so tired of bringing them up that they were leaving them down there and just picking up the gold. I had to go back and rework those holes because they were doing these things.

After about the tenth day of diving, I found the first emerald and brought it up. It was uncut, about half the size of a ping pong ball—pretty big. I showed it around and all the divers said, "Gee, we thought that was green glass. We've been finding them for days and leaving them on the bottom!" That's the truth. I had told them to bring up anything that looked suspicious. But to them those uncut emeralds and diamonds looked like broken bottles, so they were leaving them behind.

We found some big anchors on the wreck—there were two twenty-six-footers, a twenty-four-footer, and two twelve-footers. A tiny one turned up that was probably for the ship's longboat—or it could have been lost by a later salvor.

We were really lucky the first year working out there. During the first four months of search the weather was beautiful. We got six weeks of working on the wreck with almost perfect weather. Then finally a hurricane came along and that ended the season.

Excluding anchors or cannon, on an average day of working the wreck, we brought up about five hundred pounds of coral-encrusted iron. Until these clumps were x-rayed and cleaned, we had no idea what they contained. I had tons of this stuff in my back yard. Whenever I was bored, I'd get my hammer and chisel and tap, tap, find an emerald or some coins. It was a pastime. Whenever visitors came to the house they would say, "Take us out to your back yard and let's break up the clumps." Well, now there is nothing left to steal. It's all finished.

The water out there is really warm, but when we were working in it all day we wore rubber wet suits for protection. We also usually carried a stick that looked like a shark billy except that it was just like a gaff hook. To keep from getting blown away when the blaster was working, we simply dug this thing into the bottom and pivoted on it, swinging around three hundred and sixty degrees and grabbed the goodies at the same time.

One day we found the top and pieces to an enormous jar over six feet high. Scattered nearby were a lot of human bones. It seems that two nobles had died in Lima and their remains were being shipped back to be buried at the Cathedral of Valladolid. We had found their bones and the container they were in.

The captain called any precious stones jellybeans, and every-time they would come up he'd dance a jig. He actually had a jellybean jar for candy that he filled up with green emeralds, diamonds, and things like that. He was really happy. It was a lot more interesting than fishing.

Usually four guys were on the bottom while the other four were aboard the boat holding the lines, because everytime you moved to blast another hole you had to change all four anchor lines. One guy had the task of cataloguing: counting coins and keeping track of everything. It was a lot easier if the coins were in clumps, because all you had to do was weigh them. The loose ones took a lot of time. We put the coins in zip-lock plastic bags to keep them damp until they could be preserved. Otherwise they would dry out, the outer crust of silver sulphide would fall off, and a lot of detail of the coins would be lost.

On an average it took about ten to fifteen minutes to blast down to bedrock, then we did the slow fanning for another half an hour to get the rest of the sand out of the pockets. Then it would take about an hour to do all the plotting and photography. On an average it took two to two and a half hours to work every sixty-foot diameter hole. And as I said, this wreck was spread out over several square miles, so there is years of work out there.

We found quite a few complete swords and hundreds of sword hilts and parts of swords. Some were Toledo steel; others were silver dress swords. We got into the galley area and found lots of big cooking pots and pans and tons of crockery.

The reason this ship was called the Plate Wreck was because almost everything on it was silver. There were stacks of silver plates, silverware, silver salt cellars, *et cetera*. On most wrecks you find a lot of pewter, which I love to clean and study the hallmarks. But on the *Maravilla* we only found two pieces of pewter. Everything else was silver or gold; the former is harder to clean than pewter. And the gold is the easiest of all. When you find gold it actually shines. Nothing happens to it. Only occasionally we find a little silver sulphide on gold when it is near a silver coin.

We had asked the Bahamians to send out one of their people to keep an eye on their twenty-five percent of the treasure. But no one showed up for the first couple weeks. So I finally got a fast Sea Bird boat that Bascomb ran. It went thirty-five knots. Every day before sundown we would transfer the stuff as we found it from the small boat to the big boat to the Sea Bird and it was run to Fort Pierce and put in various banks until we finally ended up taking it to the Bahamas. Many times when Bascomb was going back, he would have to run through a bunch of pirates who were always waiting there to meet him. But Bascomb had a faster boat and he made it every time. He didn't always hit the right part of the coast, but he managed to reach land somehow. And by doing this he was able to bring out fresh fruit and vegetables all the time.

The bronze cannons were really interesting because they were some of the most ornate I have ever seen. I've looked at them all over the world in museums and forts. These had three coats of arms: those of Philip the Fourth, king of Spain; the Catholic church; and the Marques de Lagones, a Gentleman of the Bedchamber of Philip the Fourth who had donated the money for all of those cannon. The guns were dated 1651, 1652, and 1653, and they also had on them the name of the Dutch founder and a Latin prayer. Everything was covered with a green patina, which, when tapped, fell right off.

One of our divers had a little difficulty keeping track of uncut emeralds. The first time he found an emerald he lost it. The second time he found one he put it in his mouth and accidentally swallowed it. It took two quarts of prune juice to get it back. After that he put them in his face mask and came up that way.

Finally, right at the end, the Bahamians came. They wanted to make sure that they got their share. At this time we had three different pirate boats anchored about a mile offshore, either waiting for us to leave so that they could jump on the wreck or waiting to come over and take over one night. The worst part was diving all day and then having to keep watch at night to see that nobody would sneak on board and throw us overboard. So the Bahamians sent this enormous boat out which contained one policeman without any guns at all who was scared to death of even coming on board. So I asked him, "How are you going to protect us?" And he said, "In de name of de Queen, mon." That was before independence. Anyway, about the time one of those pirates came by to say "Goodbye, Marx, we're going back to Florida," the Bahamian jumped overboard and started swimming for his motorboat. We picked him up and took him there and he left.

You probably read about all the difficulty we had with the Bahamians over the ownership of the wreck. Who owns it? The Spanish government thinks they own it now. And to date we really haven't made a penny. So far about three to five million bucks has come up off the wreck and nobody has made a penny because everything is tied up in courts and battles.

8 ~~~~

Robert Stenuit: Going for the Girona

A dark-haired, slender young man with a trim mustache and Gallic features, Robert Stenuit was born in Brussels, Belgium, in 1932. Educated at Brussels University, he majored in political and diplomatic sciences. But having acquired an early interest in diving and shipwreck exploration, Stenuit chose to seek his fortune underwater rather than follow a political or diplomatic career. Like so many other young divers, he was first attracted to wreck hunting by the adventure it offered and the seeming simplicity of finding a fortune in treasure on the ocean floor. At the age of eighteen he started a file of lost shipwrecks. Today that file fills an entire room.

Stenuit has participated in the search for Spanish shipwrecks off the coasts of Ireland and Spain and in the investigations of Greek vessels that foundered off the coast of Sicily. As a professional diver he has worked as a marine consultant to a large oil company involved in offshore seabed drilling for oil and has participated in deep ocean dives for Edwin Link and his Man in Sea Project.

A growing interest in underwater archaeology took Stenuit to the archives of Europe, which in turn provided him with the information he needed to successfully salvage several period shipwrecks. What is particularly noteworthy about this man is his exceptional ability as a historical researcher. Not merely content with learning the location of a shipwreck, which he then manages to salvage in a proper archaeological manner, Stenuit pursues the history of his recovered artifacts through a mind-boggling maze of historical records until he learns details about the long-dead owners of the artifacts themselves. This Holmesian sleuthery is Stenuit's forte; he excels at it. It is this talent, plus the ability to write well about his experiences, that places Robert Stenuit in a special league shared by few others in his field.

In July 1588, the formidable Spanish Armada, consisting of 130 ships, 2,431 pieces of ordnance, and 8,000 men, sailed out of the port of Coruna, Spain, with the intention of sweeping across the English Channel and attacking England. The fleet was an imposing sight. One historian described it as resembling a town on the march beneath clouds of white sails emblazoned with the red Jerusalem cross. Sixty-five of the vessels were high bow and stern-decked galleons and armed merchantmen; twenty-five were stockily built cargo vessels carrying horses, mules, and provisions. Thirty-two were small pataches, patrol craft; four were galleys, small, oared gunboats; and four were galleasses, a cross between a galleon and a galley, with fifteen oarsmen on each side. Slaves and convicts chained in place, seven to an oar, provided the galleass's power. For this reason the oar-propelled gunboats were highly maneuverable, when compared to the other vessels that were entirely dependent upon the vagaries of the wind.

The fleet was led by Don Alonso Perez de Guzman el Bueno, Duke of Medina Sidonia. Under his command were 27,500 men, of which 16,000 were soldiers, 8,000 sailors, 2,000 convicts and galley slaves, and 1,500 gentlemen adventurers. Among the distinguished captains under the Duke of Medina Sidonia was Don

Alonso Martinez de Lieva, one of Spain's bravest and most famous heroes. So outstanding was his reputation that forty sons from some of the most distinguished families of Spain had volunteered to seek their fortune under his leadership. When the fleet sailed, each of the men were aboard his flagship, *La Rata Sancta Maria Encoronada*, with the soul intention of following their hero to victory over the heretic Protestants of England. But fate in the form of unfavorable weather and the wily English fleet under such stalwarts as Howard, Drake, Hawkins, and Frobisher, wreaked havoc among the vessels of the Spanish Armada. Suffering severe losses of both ships and men in engagements with the English off the coast of Calais, Medina Sidonia was forced to lead the remnants of the Armada back to Spain by way of a highly treacherous and circuitous route. He attempted to take them around England, Scotland, and Ireland—a distance of 750 leagues (2,250 miles)— through stormy seas where they knew little of the obstacles they would encounter.

Hardly half of the fleet made it home from this tortuous trip. One by one ships left their hulks ravaged on the reefs, points, and rocky crags of the rugged Scottish-Irish coast. Others foundered at sea, lost forever in the storms of that turbulent autumn.

La Rata, the flagship of the fleet, fared no better than the others. Damaged and dismasted by weeks of storms, she drifted through the north Atlantic until finally Martinez de Lieva beached her in a sheltered cove on Ireland's coast. The commander saw to it that the survivors were taken ashore along with the vessel's treasure and small arms. The *Rata* was then burned to the water level. Fortunately for the survivors, not long afterward another Armada ship, *La Duquesa Santa Ana*, picked them up and they continued their journey, only to sail this ship onto another hidden rock. Again De Lieva moved the survivors ashore with their goods and treasure, this time to establish themselves in a nearby ruined castle. Shortly thereafter the commander received word that eleven miles down the coast three other Spanish ships had come ashore. Rounding up his people, De Lieva led them to the site, where he found three vessels, two of them wrecked beyond repair and the third, the galleass *Girona*, damaged but not yet a total loss. De Lieva and his men set about repairing the *Girona*, jury-rigging her broken rudder, patching her hull, and making the vessel once more seaworthy.

When everything was ready, he took on all the crewmen, including those of the two previously wrecked vessels, and the noblest of the survivors, crowding thirteen hundred people aboard like cattle.

Once again the *Girona* set sail and once again misfortune struck the unfortunate Spaniards. On the dark, stormy night of October 26, storm-driven waves smashed the *Girona's* jury-rigged rudder, and about midnight, the wallowing galleass smashed open her hull on a submerged rock, casting the thirteen hundred souls into the turbulent sea. In a short while it was all over. Of the thirteen hundred people, only nine survived. The ship was battered to pieces on the rocky coast.

As time passed, details of the disaster were forgotten for the next 380 years, until one individual began to take more than passing interest in the fate of the *Girona*. He was Robert Stenuit.

Interestingly, Stenuit's early aspiration to become a treasure hunter was stimulated by an author who I knew had been responsible for stimulating at least three other individuals into traveling the treasure trail. It was not Robert Louis Stevenson and his *Treasure Island*, as one might suspect; it was H. E. Rieseberg, author of *I Dive for Treasure* (R. M. McBride & Co., New York, 1942). Stenuit says that he discovered Rieseberg in 1952, when he was nineteen and a student of politics in Brussels. He calls the author an American fiction writer, which he indeed was. But few of us who read him thought so at the time. As far as we knew Rieseberg was a bonafide treasure hunter who often had hand-to-tentacle fights with giant octopuses over chests of treasure he was always about to recover from shipwrecks in the South Seas.

In later years Rieseberg wrote of old Port Royal, the city that sank into the sea during an earthquake in 1692. Rieseberg told how he walked down the cobblestone streets of that sunken city in his helmet and hose diving gear and heard the mournful tolling of the cathedral bell as it swayed in the ocean currents. That story alone brought more than one diver to Jamaica searching for the

Map showing the location of the wreck of the Girona *and adjoining landmarks on the rugged coast of Northern Ireland.*

sunken riches of old Port Royal.

It was not long after the advent of the Aqua-Lung that a generation of starry-eyed treasure hunters learned that Rieseberg was indeed a fiction writer, albeit an enthralling one. So it was he who had captured Stenuit's imagination and made the young man determined to someday become a deepsea diver and go on treasure hunting expeditions of his own. The day Stenuit put down Rieseberg's book, he initiated his budding treasure hunting career by filling in his first file card on a shipwreck.

Stenuit's first wreck-related expedition took place in 1954 at Vigo Bay on the west coast of Spain, when he and other adventurers donned diving gear and went in search of the lost fleet of Spanish treasure galleons that sank there in 1702. At the time Stenuit could not think of any more fascinating way of life than becoming a treasure hunter. So he quit his studies at the university and launched himself full time into the nebulous profession. Two years of failure later had not dampened his enthusiasm for the hunt, but they left him a bit wiser about the realities of treasure hunting.

After a few more unsuccessful expeditions, Stenuit took time off to become a professional diver in 1964. More unsuccessful treasure hunts followed, and in the early 1960s he was also actively involved in exploring caves both above and below the water. To finance these various expeditions, Stenuit took a job as an adviser for a large oil company engaged in offshore seabed drilling for oil. Throughout this period Stenuit was explanding his files on treasure wrecks. And it was during a third expedition to find the treasure galleons of Vigo Bay in 1968 that he first heard of the *Girona*.

This particular expedition was led by writer–treasure hunter John Potter, who at that time was revising a manuscript he had written titled *The Treasure Diver's Guide*. In it Stenuit read about the *Girona*. The stirring tale had all the elements that had so fascinated him earlier with the romance of treasure hunting. By now Stenuit had a really severe case of treasure hunting fever. Even Potter tried to warn him of the possible consequences by quoting him Joseph Conrad: "There is no way to escape from a treasure, once it fastens itself upon your mind." But Stenuit was already too far gone.

So anxious was he to find the *Girona* that he started researching the subject before he left Spain. Getting what information he could from the libraries and museums in Madrid, he moved on to others in Brussels, Paris, and Holland, painstakingly gathering an enormous amount of material about the Spanish Armada—but

very little about the *Girona*. Meanwhile his job with the oil company took him off for a year in South America and two years in
North America.

In the United States he joined Ocean Systems Corporation
and worked with Edwin A. Link during his Man in Sea Project, in
which Stenuit's team spent two days and two nights living and
working 430 feet beneath the sea off the Bahamas. Then he was
sent back to England to supervise the company's London office.
Despite a tight schedule, Stenuit managed to spend three hours a
night, three nights a week, continuing his *Girona* research in the
reading rooms of the British Museum or the Public Records
Office. In the next year and a half he spent some six hundred
hours gathering bits and pieces of information relating to the fate
of the *Girona*. Everything ever written about the Armada in
England or Ireland came under his scrutiny until finally he narrowed his search down to the statements of nine noted Armada
historians.

Each of the nine historians put the loss of the *Girona* somewhere along a four-mile stretch of wild Northern Ireland coast
bounded on the west by the remains of Dunluce Castle and on the
east by Benbane Head. Five of the historians said the *Girona*
struck a rock and went down at, near, or within sight of Dunluce
Castle. The others said she sank at, or within sight of the Giant's
Causeway, a solidified lava flow, or that it had wrecked on the
Rock of Bunboys.

One look at a contemporary map, and Stenuit realized that
most of the historian's statements were contradictory. One said
that the ship struck a rock near the Giant's Causeway and went
down off Dunluce Castle. The two places were at least three miles
apart. Another historian said she was driven ashore at Dunluce . . .
at a point known ever since as Port na Spaniagh. Again, on the
modern map, these two places were separated by several miles.
Still another historian contradicted himself when he said, "She was
wrecked on the rock of Bunboys. . . ." Elsewhere he wrote, "The
bay is smaller than Port Ballintrae where the *Girona* foundered. . . ."

What was Stenuit to believe? Where was the Rock of Bunboys? It did not appear under that name on his modern map.

Back to the reading rooms he went. He found the name on the old charts under several different spellings: Bunbois, Bon Boys, and, on a sixteenth-century chart, he found Boys River located midway between Dunluce and the Giant's Causeway. On the contemporary map it was named Bush River. In an Irish-English glossary in a pilot book, Stenuit learned that Bun meant estuary. Bois translated to Bush. Thus, the rock of Bunbois was the rock of Bush estuary, or Bushfoot as it was called on his modern map.

Another document stated that the said galley ". . . struck against the rock of Bunboyes, where both ship and men perished, save only five who hardly got to shore. . . . This rock of Bunboyes is hard by Sorley Boy's house."

Sorley Boy's house was actually Dunluce Castle, owned at that time by the local lord, Sorley Boy McDonnell, who hated the English. Further searching revealed that English officials in Ireland reported that not only had some of the Spanish survivors made it to Dunluce Castle, where they were helped by Sorley Boy McDonnell, but some time after the wreck, Sorley Boy's son, James, supposedly salvaged three cannon and three chests of treasure from the wreck. Two years later he renovated and enlarged the castle. Stenuit could guess where his newfound wealth had come from.

All evidence pointed to the site of the wreck being this rock off Bush River, about two miles from Dunluce. But others had made the same deduction. All the early searchers had scoured the ocean's depths around the rock and found nothing.

Another thing bothered Stenuit. All the sixteenth-century maps of the area showed only Dunluce and the River Bois. None of the adjacent points and coves were named, as they were on his modern map. Why were such places as Spaniard Rock, Spaniard Cave, Port na Spaniagh, and Lacada Point all missing from the older maps? Certainly they had something to do with the Spanish shipwreck in the area.

Stenuit reexamined the facts. Sorley Boy and James McDonnell apparently knew the location of the shipwreck. They had reported it to be at Bunboyes Rock within sight of the castle. But had the McDonnells really pinpointed the place that easily for their hated English lords? Or had they instead fabricated the story to throw the English off? Since nobody had ever found any trace of a wreck around Bunboyes Rock, that possibility sounded more logical to Stenuit. It might also explain why only the modern maps had named places that were obviously associated with the Spanish wreck. Was it because the descendants of the McDonnells had never revealed their names for these secret places along their coast until at least ten generations had passed and there was no longer any need to conceal them? Then, when a surveyor asked the local people what the points and coves were called, he was given the names that had been passed down by word of mouth for the last two hundred years.

At least Stenuit thought it was a good theory. It still did not give him the location of the wreck, but he suspected that it had more to do with those Spanish coastal names than did Bunboys Rock off the mouth of Bush River. So, of the three remaining names, Port na Spaniagh struck Stenuit as a more likely spot to expect to find the *Girona*. At least, he thought, it would not hurt to go there and look.

Accompanied by his long time friend, Belgian photographer Marc Jasinski, Stenuit went to Ireland and found the place they were interested in. When they saw it on that stormy day in June 1967, all they felt was a strong misgiving. They asked themselves how anyone could expect to find a trace of wreckage after four hundred years on that godforsaken coast. The Giant's Causeway consisted of huge prism-shaped columns of cracked lava stacked high beside the storm-tossed Atlantic. Port na Spaniagh was a devil's cauldron of angry seas smashing into vertical black cliffs four hundred feet high. If this was where the handful of survivors managed to make shore, Stenuit understood why 1,291 others from the *Girona* had perished that dark stormy night.

Several days later when the storm abated, Stenuit and Jasinski loaded an inflatable dinghy with scuba gear and motored out from Portballintrae down the coast to examine the bottom around Port na Spaniagh.

They anchored their boat near an underwater rock off the

cove, and Stenuit donned diving gear and went over the side. The water was frigid, but he had worn his wetsuit to ward off the chill. Thirty feet beneath him the bottom consisted of large jumbled boulders often hidden by thick strands of undulating kelp. Stenuit first explored two nearby rock reefs, thinking that they were logical places for the *Girona* to end its days. But he found nothing. Following his compass, he moved across the bottom, stopping now and then to turn over a rock. Still nothing. Not the slightest trace of anything that might have belonged to the four-hundred-year-old wreck.

Finally reaching the cliff base of Lacada Point, Stenuit skirted it and moved out onto a stone platform. And there, sitting by itself, was a gray lump that looked strangely out of place. It was a three-foot-long lead ingot. When Stenuit recognized it his heart leaped. He knew Spanish ships carried items such as this for ballast. He heaved the block over, and there was the confirmation of his suspicions: five Jerusalem crosses stamped on its upper face. Stenuit had found the *Girona's* grave. A feeling of joy surged through him.

He swam down the corridor before him and encountered a bronze cannon slightly longer than his outstretched arms protruding from the rocks. Continuing down the sloping rock-strewn gully, he came upon another gun, a breechloader inscribed with the Spanish coat of arms. Nearby lay a couple breechblocks, then another ingot of lead and cannonballs haphazardly strewn all over the bottom. Stenuit was overwhelmed with the sudden wealth of finds. Not a museum in the world owned a cannon—or for that matter even a cannonball—from the Spanish Armada. And here he was, literally surrounded by them!

Back at the boat, Jasinski guessed what was behind Stenuit's grin even before he blurted out that he had found the wreck.

Three days of storms followed before they could return to the wreck. This time Jasinski went down with Stenuit to photograph the finds. After showing him the ingot, Stenuit picked up a gray pebble with the intention of pretending to his friend that he had found a piece of eight. But as Stenuit turned the object over in his hand, he was amazed to see that it was indeed a silver coin, badly worn but quite clearly stamped with the Jerusalem cross. Elated, the two divers shook hands and congratulated each other in a welter of bubbles.

Stenuit began digging around the lead ingot he had first found. Before long he had collected another piece of eight, a few links of gold chain, and a tiny gold ring. More cannonballs appeared, but as a result of the recent storms the fully exposed bronze cannon was now half buried beneath sand.

Meanwhile Jasinski explored closer to shore, working around the cove before Spaniard Cave and checking the sea bottom around Spaniard Rock. He found nothing. Moving into deeper water, farther out than Stenuit, he came upon a large anchor measuring well over six feet from fluke to fluke. Had it once belonged to the *Girona*? They assumed that it had.

By day's end, when the treasure hunters considered what they had accomplished, it became evident that they needed more sophisticated excavating equipment: something to move large boulders aside so that they could look beneath them; something to shift and sift some four thousand cubic feet of sand, gravel, and rocks to reach the best finds. It would take time and money, a combination that they would not be able to get together until the following year.

By the next April they were once again operational as a well equipped treasure hunting team. This time they had done some planning. Unlike many treasure hunters solely interested in pillaging a wreck site for its treasure, Stenuit wanted to work the site in a proper archaeological manner. This meant taking care to record the proper placement of all wreck objects and their relationship to each other so that a proper plan could be made of the site for whatever archaeological information might be learned from the scattered pieces of the puzzle. Joining Stenuit and Jasinski this time were professional French divers Maurice Vidal and Louis Gorsse. Stenuit, who had gotten a leave of absence, had found a sponsor in friend Henri Delauze, a Marseille diver who furnished the necessary equipment. Stenuit and the others were financing the expedition themselves until they were later helped generously by a grant from the National Geographic Society. After that, work progressed whenever weather permitted along the frequently stormbound coast.

The uneven bottom made the laying of a grid difficult. Instead, the divers stretched rope from one landmark to another, establishing an underwater network within which they tagged items, carefully photographed them in place, then brought them up for preservation. The photography and preservation of the artifacts were Jasinski's job. Francis Dumont, an architectural student, sketched the finds and drew the chart.

Assuming correctly that all heavy objects would seek their lowest level in this constantly shifting sand bottom, the divers went to work clearing away the overburden with a water jet operating from a pump in the dinghy. The strong column of water blasted away the rocks and pebbles of the upper layers, then ate rapidly through the finer sand and chalk beneath until bedrock was reached and blown clean. Then they moved in with their crevicing tools, digging down into the cracks and coming up with lead, iron and pewter, silver, gold, and bejeweled items that had settled there so long before. Every inch of the bottom was carefully searched in this manner. Then it was necessary to raise two of the cannon to see what might lie beneath them. The heavy bronze tubes came up easily enough, suspended from big neoprene bags filled with air from the divers' regulators, but once these items were taken ashore, the secret was out. Local people no longer had to wonder what the divers found so interesting on the bottom of the cove. An eight-foot-long heavy bronze cannon couldn't be passed off for anything but what it was. And old Spanish cannon automatically spelled treasure.

Thereafter for a while Stenuit's men were plagued by pirates, groups of scuba divers that moved in to pirate what they could

Opposite: Among the treasure Robert Stenuit and his companions recovered from the wreck of the Girona *was a tiny winged gold salamander that once wore a row of rubies down its back (three were still there); a gold Maltese cross once belonging to a Knight of Malta, the* Girona's *captain, perhaps; and a small gilded brass dolphin perhaps used as an ornament.*

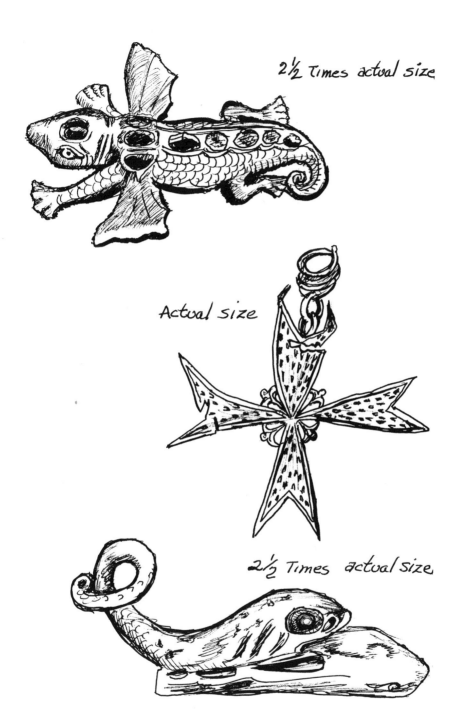

2½ Times actual size

Actual size

2½ Times actual size

right from under the noses of Stenuit's crew. Fortunately, however, Stenuit had taken the trouble to register the site with the proper authorities in London and had established himself as the proper "salvor in possession." And to make doubly sure that outsiders understood his position, he anchored a large plastic ball within the site area. On the marker was this statement:

NOTICE TO ALL DIVERS

All sunken objects within a radius of 400 yards round this buoy are under an archaeological survey being carried out by Mr. Robert Stenuit as exclusive salvor. It is strictly forbidden to tamper with any sunken objects in any way whatsoever. Immediate action will be taken in court against trespassers.

Acting as if they had not seen the sign, the diving pirates moved in on the site. The immediate action taken by the "salvor in possession" and his assistants amounted to an underwater confrontation in which any articles picked up by the pirates were quickly snatched out of their hands by the salvors, to the accompaniment of much finger-wagging, head-shaking, and disgruntled bubblings. With persistence, Stenuit and his men beat off all enemy advances and retreated from the field of battle with their site more or less intact.

The difficulty of the search was to ferret out the smallest items of value in all that bottom rubble. Excavating great masses of rocky overburden and digging down through the next layers often resulted in the discovery of perhaps six tiny links of gold chain—not a large return for the amount of effort expended. But the divers soon learned that thanks to the peculiarities of tidal currents and ocean eddies, the sea sometimes concentrated artifacts in rather unexpected places. Once aware of this they were often rewarded with pockets of treasure. For example, they found what soon became known as Treasure Cave, two slabs of rock supported in the middle by a few stone pillars and in front by round boulders. Enough tantalizing artifacts appeared just under the edge of the rocks to suggest that this might be one of the major deposits. Hot on the treasure trail, the divers dug down under the slabs, bucketing out tons of gravel until they had burrowed themselves completely underneath. Still the artifacts appeared. They found that the left side of their manmade cave was a gold mine, while the right side was a silver mine. But with every foot of progress, the hazards of their position increased. To get at the tormentingly elusive pieces, they had to take more chances, further jeopardizing their safety. Still the trail led on, enticing them further.

They chipped away carefully at the pillars of empacked rocks supporting the stone roof to reach a silver inkwell or a length of gold chain. With equal caution they removed the underlaying foundation of the supports to pick up a trail of silver coins. The more intense the effort became, the more aware they were of their precarious position. If either diver loosened the wrong key stone the two-hundred-ton slabs balanced overhead would slam down, smashing them flatter than pancakes.

They continued cautiously with the excavation, sweating out the removal of each supportive pebble now. So critical did it finally become that at one point Stenuit said he saw a silver candlestick jammed under a little stone resting on a larger stone that supported the two-hundred-ton roof. With utmost care, while keeping one eye on the way out, Stenuit reached out with a crowbar and dislodged the small stone. Something scraped, and the next thing he knew he was outside the cave looking in, not sure how he got there so fast but relieved to see that his cave-burrowing companion, Maurice Vidal, had reacted with equal alacrity and was right there beside him, peering back sheepishly at their cave burrow, the roof of which surprisingly still stood. Each man pantomimed an admonishment to the other for moving the wrong stone. Then they returned to their cave and picked up where they had left off.

By the next day Stenuit was able to extricate the difficult candlestick. The only trouble was that in the hole it left he could just see the sheen of another candlestick buried beneath it. He had to have the pair. He got them, then spotted a plate, next a gem, then a glitter of gold . . .

Somehow the divers accomplished the improbable; they excavated the entire thing without the slightest mishap. As Stenuit later reported, "The cave is still there, scraped down to the last wrinkle of the last crevice of the last cranny. And no one left any bones behind. The slab is hanging there suspended in the water, defying gravity, a monument to our temerity."

Gradually the finds accumulated into a tidy pile. Along with a great many cannonballs, including many made of stone, and parts of the ship's ordnance, the divers found smashed gold goblets, up to ten gold coins a day, bits and pieces of jewelry, a bent gold Cross of Malta medal, and from under the slabs of rock, perhaps one of the most unusual pieces of jewelry: a winged gold salamander with each scale clearly engraved, a row of rubies inset down its back. One afternoon, in less than an hour, Stenuit filled a jam jar, a mustard jar, and a Band-Aid can with pieces of silver and gold he picked from the pebbles of the bottom. At least for the moment their rich glow almost made up for all the time he had spent poring over the research books, all the days they had spent fighting the strong currents, enduring the discomfort of the constant bone-chilling water, the stiff joints, aching muscles, the untold hours of measuring, recovering, charting, cleaning, preserving, and recording their finds. Still it was not over.

The bottom-altering, back-breaking work continued throughout the summer. As the water warmed the kelp growth increased, occasioning more work in clearing large sections of the area before the jetting, sifting, fanning took place in the endless search for every last item from the wreck. Interestingly, not a bit of wood remained from the great galleass, all of it having been long ago consumed by the boring organisms of the sea. Nor did the divers find remnants of the chains or leg-irons that had kept the hundreds of slaves at their oars even as the ship tore asunder and went down—at least no recognizable iron objects had appeared. But underlying much of the bottom was a matrix made up of many unidentifiable fragments of the wreck. Almost everything was now reduced to a kind of ferrous oxide amalgam, all packed together into a nameless conglomerate. Only an occasional humble medal of pewter bearing the image of Christ and the Virgin Mary suggested to the divers that they might have found what once belonged to the unfortunate galley slaves, who perhaps were clutching them even as they went to the bottom weighted down by their chains.

During the last days of the search it seemed the divers turned up their most exquisite finds. One day a diver found a beautifully tooled gold broach framed in pearls. A couple days later, while searching beneath a large boulder, Stenuit found an exquisitely carved lapis lazuli cameo set in an ornate gold frame decorated with eight pearls. The cameo was a Roman emperor's head in profile. In another three hours of patient burrowing and sifting he recovered three more similar broaches, each with a different Roman emperor's profile represented on the cameo. And then, the most poignant find of all, a small delicate woman's gold ring shaped like two tiny hands, one clasping a heart, the other a belt buckle. Around the outside of the band the Spanish inscription read, *"No tengo mas que darte*—I have nothing more to give thee."* Stenuit wondered if it had been given to some young Spanish nobleman by his betrothed as he gallantly sailed off with the Armada to conquer England.

In late September, with nothing more to be found, the team called a halt to their search. While the *Girona* was no treasure galleon, it had produced a significant amount of valuable artifacts, including numerous gold rings, medallions, buttons, broaches, a gold chain, bits of pottery, candlesticks, cannon, lead ingots and balls, an astrolabe and navigational dividers, tiny quartz perfume bottles with silver stoppers, and one hundred and forty gold and six hundred silver coins. In addition, it yielded a considerable amount of archaeological data that now could be assembled, studied, analyzed, and interpreted to form a major piece of information that had been missing from this particular historical puzzle for over three hundred and fifty years. Thanks to the efforts of Robert Stenuit and his team of divers, that piece is now in place.

9 ～～～

ROBERT STENUIT: SILVER OF THE SLOT TER HOOGE

In November 1724, the *Slot ter Hooge*, a huge square-rigged merchant ship belonging to the Dutch East India Company, left the Netherlands heading for the Dutch East Indies. Stacked in chests in her hold were three tons of silver ingots and coins destined for use in the sprawling East Indian trade. As the ship made its way south along the coast of Portugal, it was struck by a savage Atlantic gale that drove her helplessly off course into the Madeira Islands. In the middle of the night she hit treacherous rocks off the small island of Porto Santo that ripped open her hull and strewed her precious cargo across the bottom of the ocean. In that night of horror, 221 of her passengers perished; only 33 survived.

Shortly after the disaster, an enterprising Englishman named John Lethbridge was hired by the East India Company to salvage what he could of the *Slot ter Hooge*'s treasure.

Lethbridge was far ahead of his time. About 1715 he had

built a kind of diving bell resembling an elongated barrel large enough to hold a man. The diver entered the contraption through a hatch on top which was then bolted in place. He slipped his arms out through two holes waterproofed by well-greased leather sleeves tied tightly around his biceps. A four-inch-wide and a quarter-inch-thick glass window in front of his face enabled him to see out. Ballasted by iron castings, the device was suspended horizontally on a cable from a surface vessel. History tells us that Lethbridge was successful in using this diving machine for salvaging treasure from numerous wrecks. So he was the most logical person for the Dutch East India Company to contact in the hope that he could salvage something of value from the *Slot ter Hooge.*

And there the story ended. Robert Stenuit had stumbled onto this account of the *Slot ter Hooge* during his early research in the Dutch archives. But since the records failed to report the precise location of the wreck, or even whether or not Lethbridge had been successful in salvaging anything from it, he was unable to do anything. He was stopped by the same lack of information that had thwarted many another treasure hunter before him. So he simply filed away the data he had until another time.

After Stenuit's success in finding the *Girona,* he once again turned to the problem of the *Slot ter Hooge.* When he queried the archivists at The Hague for more information, they merely shook their heads and said they had no further records available. The documents were either lost, destroyed, or forgotten among the many thousands of similar records as yet uncatalogued.

Stenuit searched elsewhere, digging for possible scraps of overlooked information about the *Slot ter Hooge* in various European archives. Then, by a strange quirk of luck, he learned what he wanted to know. It was not a forgotten document that tipped him off to the location of the long lost wreck; it was a chance coincidence that had all the elements of the best treasure hunting fiction tale.

While visiting two other wreck hunter–historians interested in researching period shipwrecks, Stenuit was shown a historical society document from 1880 that discussed a silver tankard on which were engraved two remarkable pictures. While the tankard

itself had long ago been lost, Stenuit was intrigued by the sketch of
the engravings. One showed without a doubt a crude picture of
John ·Lethbridge's diving machine suspended from a vessel full
of salvagers. The other engraving was of an island with the words,
"Porto Santo Island, Lat. 33-N Lon. 5." And in a northern notch
of that island was the unmistakable picture of a sailing vessel sinking. A monogram identified the tankard as having belonged to
Lethbridge himself.

Stenuit was tremendously excited over the discovery. Porto
Santo was in the Madeira Islands. Did this engraving depict the
resting place of the long lost *Slot ter Hooge?* If so, it was as good as
a bona fide treasure map with a big X marking the spot where the
treasure was hidden.

Making a copy of the engraving, Stenuit flew to The Hague,
where he made arrangements with the Dutch government to salvage the vessel for 75 percent of whatever he found. The remaining 25 percent would go to the Dutch government. Then Stenuit
headed for the National Library of Portugal in Lisbon. Studying
eighteenth- and nineteenth-century charts of the Madeira Islands,
he learned that the modern name of the bay on the north coast of
Porto Santo Island was Porto do Guilherme. The Portuguese government agreed to allow Stenuit to work the wreck without any
recompense for whatever treasure he might find.

Despite the possibility of the *Slot ter Hooge* being in the bay,
Stenuit was plagued with uncertainty. Should he launch a costly
expedition with the possibility that John Lethbridge had already
salvaged the bulk of the treasure, indeed perhaps all of it?

Back he went to the national archives in The Hague. Since
his previous visit there new records had been catalogued. Again
Lady Luck smiled on him. With trembling fingers, Stenuit leafed
through documents detailing Lethbridge's agreement with the
Dutch East India Company and his salvage effort on the *Slot ter
Hooge.* The company had contracted Lethbridge to do the salvage
in 1725, hardly a year after the ship had gone down. It appeared
that the Englishman had been quite successful. On his first dive in
the bay he had recovered 349 of the 1500 missing silver bars, along
with most of the pieces of eight, over 9,000 Dutch guilders worth

of smaller coins, and two cannon. Lethbridge assured his employ-
ers that he could fish up much more if he could just get twenty or
thirty days of calm weather. Apparently he did because the second
time he visited the wreck the documents stated that he recovered a
sum equal to more than half of the *Slot ter Hooge*'s recorded
treasure. After that the returns slowly diminished. Breaking off his
salvage of the wreck for five years, Lethbridge returned there
again in 1732 but only recovered enough to partly fill a small chest.
Additional attempts in 1733 and 1734 resulted in the recovery of
little more. Doing some deft figuring, Stenuit concluded that
Lethbridge had left between 100 and 251 silver bars on the wreck
that he had failed to recover—enough to make it definitely worthwhile for Stenuit to start his search.

Backed financially by the National Geographic Society and a
French undersea engineering group known as COMEX, Stenuit
rounded up his expedition. The diving team consisted of Louis
Gorsse, Alan Fink, Michel Gangloff, and Roger Perquin. Arriving
at the island of Porto Santo that spring, the men made their way to
Porto do Guilherme and looked down from the four-hundred-foot-
high cliffs that backed the small bay. Oddly enough, the graveyard
of the *Slot ter Hooge* was very similar to that of the *Girona*, which
had gone down in a similar cliff-walled bay on the coast of Northern Ireland. Stenuit saw easily how 221 passengers could have
perished trying to make it to safety against that steep rocky escarp-
ment lashed by storm waves. It was a miracle that anyone had
survived.

As he had done while surveying the site of the *Girona*,
Stenuit launched his inflatable rubber boat at a more convenient
site down the coast, and an hour later the divers dropped anchor
in sixty feet of clear water in the bay. Stenuit was the first into his
diving gear and over the side to check on his boat's mooring. And
at that moment he found the *Slot ter Hooge*'s anchor! They had
come to rest directly over it.

Again, using the same techniques that he had on the *Girona*,
he divided the site into five sections, with individual divers surveying each section. When the men reported back to the boat there
was no doubt that they were on the wreck site. The divers re-

ported finding half-buried iron cannon, lots of cannonballs, and wreckage strewn all over the bottom near the base of boulders and the cliffs.

On their next dive Stenuit found a brass swivel gun with its breechblock lying nearby, lots of barshot, the iron hoops from long-since rotted casks of brandy, a myriad of wine bottles, most of them broken but some intact right up to their corks. The first treasure that turned up was a small Dutch silver coin found beneath a broken wine bottle. It was dated 1724, the proper date for the wreck.

The divers set to work between bouts with inclement weather. Gradually the wreck began to give up its treasure, first in the form of silver coins oftentimes embedded in mounds of concretion on the bottom. Elsewhere as many as a hundred coins lay exposed on a large flat rock, indicating that probably no diver since Lethbridge had looked into this small inlet searching for treasure, because even an amateur treasure hunter would have had no difficulty recognizing the small silver-white disks for what they were.

The divers soon found that when hand-fanning patches of sand they literally turned into veins of silver. The deeper they dug the more coins they found. The buried coins had only light encrustations on them. But where were the silver ingots? wondered Stenuit. Had these heavier masses of metal worked their way to the bottom of these soft sand pockets, deeper than the rest of the lighter artifacts?

Obtaining a heavy-duty air lift and compressor from the cooperative islanders, Stenuit's team began digging deeper. And one day in mid-August the men heard the air lift *clonk* up its first silver ingot. It was a six-inch by two-inch bar with a picture of a small rose stamped on one corner, probably to indicate the degree of silver fineness.

With this first ingot the divers thought they might be into the "mother lode" but several days passed before the second ingot appeared. As the air lift burrowed deeper into the bottom, ten feet below the substrata they dug out a mass containing twenty-five silver bars fused together. Then, diver Louis Gorsse made the kind

When Robert Stenuit saw these engravings on an old silver tankard, they gave him the exact location of the long lost Slot ter Hooge. *They were as good as a bonafide treasure map with a big X marking the spot where the treasure lay hidden.*

of find that treasure hunters dream about. Tapping Stenuit on the shoulder one day, he led him across the bottom to one of the ancient cannon. There wedged beneath it were the worm-eaten remains of a chest stacked full of silver bars. It was the pinnacle of the hunt for Stenuit.

Determined not to touch the unique find until he could photograph and record it in place, Stenuit cabled London for his friend and expert photographer Marc Jasinski, who arrived from Belgium a few days later. Unfortunately, Jasinski was never to see the chest as it was originally found. By the time a few more days had elapsed a storm passed and word got out that the group had found the chest. When he and Stenuit went back to photograph it they found that a thief had beat them to it. Someone had smashed the chest and removed all but fifteen of the silver ingots, leaving behind a telltale orange snorkel that belonged to none of the team members.

Stenuit was furious with himself for his carelessness. The only photographs he had of the original chest were those he had made shortly after its discovery. He felt that no one on the island of Porto Santo was either dishonest enough or skilled enough to pull off the theft. Instead he suspected that it might be a group of young divers from Madeira Island. A few days later, by diplomatically approaching the wife of the group's leader, subtle threats of exposure were made that resulted in the individual returning the stolen bars of silver to one of the local authorities.

As the summer drew to a close, so too did Stenuit's salvage work on the *Slot ter Hooge*. His charts of the finds showed telltale scatter patterns that indicated what had happened during the East Indiaman's final death throes. Driven onto the rocks on the west side of the bay by the ferocity of the storm, she had been disembowled, strewing brick and tile ballast, lead pigs, casks, bottles, cannon, and cannonballs all over the bottom at the initial impact site. Ripping free of the rocks, she drifted eastward to the opposite side of the stone-walled amphitheater, spilling treasure and cargo along the way until she was smashed to smithereens against a great cleft of rock, her remains scattered to oblivion by the surging seas.

In winding up his work at the inlet, Stenuit was pleased that John Lethbridge had not only left them a share of the treasure but also a good cross-section of seventeenth- and eighteenth-century artifacts that would surely provide historians with additional information about the period. Once again the treasure hunter archaeologist had combined equal measures of diligent research, detective persistence, and hard work—topped with a dash of good luck—to concoct his special recipe for success.

10 ~~~~

Treasure Salvors: Search for the Atocha
Part One

On the morning of September 4, 1622, twenty-eight vessels of the *Armada de Tierra Firma* and the *Tierra Firma Flota*, commanded by the Marquis de Caldereita, sailed from Havana bound for Spain. Two days later in the Florida Straits the treasure fleet was struck by a severe tropical storm. High winds ripped away sails and rigging, scattering the ships from the Florida Keys to the Dry Tortugas. A week later, most of the storm-scarred vessels made it back to Havana. The rest had either gone down at sea or been driven onto shoals with a heavy loss of lives. Among the missing vessels were three warships—the *Santa Margarita*, the *Nuestra Señora del Rosario*, and the *Nuestra Señora de Atocha*—which had carried the bulk of the treasure. The *Atocha* alone was loaded with over a million pesos of registered silver bullion and specie. Spanish salvors soon found and recovered everything of value off the galleon *La Rosario,* stranded on one of the keys in the Dry Tortugas. They also located the wreck of the *Atocha* with only her mizzen mast sticking out of the water. The sunken ship was intact, and the Spanish divers were unable to get into the hull because hatches and ports were still battened down. Leaving a marker at the site, they went to search for the wreck of the *Margarita.* A fierce October storm drove them off. Returning to work on the *Atocha,* they found their marker missing and the wreck gone. Some of the salvors suspected that the ship had sunk into the quicksand bottom; others later reported finding half of the *Atocha*'s side washed ashore on a nearby island.

Four years later, salvors found the wreck of the *Margarita* and partially salvaged her treasure. But the *Atocha* was never seen again. For all intents and purposes, the galleon and her treasure had simply vanished into limbo. Treasure hunter estimates of her true value in unregistered bullion soar as high as $400 million. "Find the *Atocha,*" declared one underwater archaeologist, "and you will have found the second most valuable shipwreck in the western hemisphere. The first is Columbus' flagship, the *Santa Maria.*"

Three centuries of searchers failed to crack the secret of the *Atocha*'s whereabouts. Time had erased all clues. No one even remembered where the fleet foundered, let alone where one apparently intact treasure galleon had dropped out of sight just days after it went down.

In the last couple decades, however, the hunters backtracked the trail of the lost galleon into the musty archives of Spain and found nuggets of information hidden in voluminous packets of long-forgotten Spanish records. Soon bits and pieces of the story became known among the modern day treasure hunters, pointing them toward the supposed site of the lost fleet. According to the translation of a letter from the Marquis de Caldereita, commander of the fleet, he stated that the captain of the *Margarita* told him that ". . . the force of the wind and the currents pushed the galleon forward up to ten *brazas,* [sixty feet] where it grounded and was lost in the sand bank which is located on the west side of the last of the Matecumbe Keys, next to the Head of the Martires off the

Florida coast. At 7:00 A.M. of that day he saw one league [three statute miles] to the east the galleon named *Nuestra Señora de Atocha, Almiranta* of the fleet, without rigging or sails . . . and as he watched he saw it go down and sink to the bottom. . . ."

And elsewhere in the *legajos,* this statement was translated regarding a Spanish salvage effort: ". . . reaching the place where the *Almiranta Atocha* was lost, he did not see the *mesana* [mizzen mast] nor any other signs, and figuring that the October storm had destroyed it, he went to look around all the Matecumbe Keys to find some signs. On one of them he saw half the side of the *Almiranta.* . . ."

Once this translation got out, all the treasure hunters who could scrounge the equipment fell over each other scouring the ocean bottom around Florida's Matecumbe Keys, two small islands in the upper third of the Florida Keys. But all they found was lots of shallow water and no treasure wreck.

In the following interview, Mel Fisher tells of his long search for the lost *Atocha,* a tireless search involving all the intrigues, clues, setbacks, shocks, surprises, and rewards of a well-written crime novel, an obsessing search that has cost him a small fortune and the lives of four people, including his eldest son.

When did you first hear about the Atocha?

Well, I guess the first person that mentioned it to me was Captain Bob Jordan in Marathon in 1966. He said he thought it was off the Tennessee Light [southwest of Lower Matecumbe Key]. We spent a couple of days magging in deep water along the edge of the reef, about sixty feet down, but couldn't find it. We found a modern wreck, that was all.

Had you gotten any documentation about the Atocha *from the Spanish archives yet?*

No, the documentation was Potter's *Treasure Diver's Guide,* which in my opinion is an excellent work. John Potter, Junior, has done extensive research in the archives, and he has attempted to consolidate this research down to a treasure diving guidebook for guys like me around the world who want to go after treasure. He has done a mighty fine job. But in this case he made a mistake which is readily understandable. He had the *Atocha* near Alligator Light up near Islamorada. I realized that the information was rather vague and inaccurate and I did not have any good research on it. So I stopped looking for it at that time.

Were you working on the 1715s during that period?

I was working on both the 1715 and the 1733 fleets.

Winding up the 1715s?

Well, due to rough breakers and dirty water, we could only work the 1715 fleet for a period of about one hundred and twenty days in the summertime, when the water was flat and clear. So every year in the wintertime, I came down to the Keys and worked the 1733 fleet. I started another company called Armada Research just for that, to keep it separate from the Real Eight contract up there. We were very successful. We found about five hundred shipwrecks up and down the coast.

Mel Fisher with artifacts recovered from a mystery wreck in area of the Marquesas Keys. He holds an ivory tusk in his left hand and leg-irons in his right. Other items include encrusted tankard, bowls and rum bottle.

I really started hunting for the *Atocha* in 1968, when I decided to spend one hundred days out of my life looking for it. At that point I had gained some information from the archives, a few pages here and there, mentioning Matecumbe, so I figured we'd block out all of Matecumbe and mag it out. Now at that time these were not considered Florida waters. I had letters from the attorney general's office stating that the boundary was three miles from land and anything beyond that was outside the territorial limits of Florida; for me to go ahead and hunt and good luck. So I did, every day one winter for one hundred and one days.

Were you checking around Upper or Lower Matecumbe?

Both. The whole thing. And it wasn't there. I couldn't believe it.

You were running the mag patterns over this area?

Yes. Magnetometer patterns back and forth, very tight and accurate and through all kinds of weather. We were fanatics. Bobby Jordan was working with me again, and several other well-known treasure hunters. We found thirteen old galleon type ships in that area when we were looking for the *Atocha*. I would investigate them, and I knew they were not 1622 because I could recognize the different pieces of pottery and coins as being a lot of vintages. I would work on the wrecks a little, and if I lost interest I would subcontract them out to some other company to work, where we would receive one-fourth for turning the wreck over to them. I subcontracted four of these wrecks out to Tom Gurr, who at that time had a company named Marine Tech. I think one of the wrecks was part of the *Chevez*; one of them the *Tres Puentes*.

All 1733s?

Yes. Well, we're not sure that they were all 1733s, but probably. There were a couple others out there, too. I subcontracted some to other divers and companies. We went out every day in all kinds of rough weather. Whenever anything went wrong with the engines, we would work all night and get them ready by next morning. We were determined to put in twelve hours a day magging. And we did.

The thing wasn't there, so we searched all the way north, damn near to Miami . . . found more wrecks, but none of them was the *Atocha*. Then I searched south. We also use an autogyro for magging, because it can keep a stable altitude above water. We magged all the way down to American Shoals down toward Key West. And we still did not find the *Atocha*.

By then I learned from Gene Lyon in the archives that the word *Matecumbe* in those days was synonymous with the Keys. That's like saying that the *Atocha* sank in the Florida Keys. So this meant there was a huge area to search. Hundreds and hundreds of thousands of miles. I just began expanding my search through the last five years to encompass the whole thing.

About three years ago, Gene called me up from Spain and said he had found a reference to the island of Marquesas in connection with the salvage records of the *Margarita*. You see, he had to go through about six years of records before he got to the point where someone mentioned anything about it. The reason for this was that after the Spaniards abandoned any hope of finding the *Atocha* or further salvaging the *Margarita*, the king of Spain issued an order that no one was to write down the locations of these shipwrecks, because mailboats were often stopped by pirates or privateers who might learn their whereabouts.

You had by then read the statement by the captain of the Margarita *that he saw the* Atocha *going down?*

Yes, I believe I had that by then.

Was it something that Gene turned up during that period?

Gene turned up more than a thousand documents concerning the subject to me. Now we have several thousand more. As it turns out, he has researched like a hundred years of it, because even after those people [the salvagers] abandoned it others tried to find it . . . just like me. So he went through all the records of all the hunts for this and all the salvage records. We have lots of daily salvage records on the *Margarita*. We know exactly what they brought up each day because the king had four of his agents on board, just like we have a state agent on board with us today. And one of those guys even dived. So each one would keep a record of every item that came up, and that way the king knew that he was getting everything and that they were not absconding with it.

Then this clue from the Spanish archives narrowed your field of search?

Yes. When Gene gave me the idea that it was somewhere in the Marquesas area, I decided to move the whole company, lock, stock, and barrel, to Key West. It was a major decision. I decided to go all out for the *Atocha*.

After you started magging and searching for the Atocha *in the Marquesas, what was the first thing you found?*

Well, it was a big big ocean out there, and I thought it was going to be simple since we had a fair area instead of the whole Florida Keys to search. But when I got out there, I discovered for the first time that I had tried open water searching where you can't see any landmark anywhere, nothing but water in all directions—with a hell of a current going, changing directions along with the wind. It blew us all around the ocean, and we were just zigzagging around and completely lost about ninety percent of the time. So we turned on the magnetometer and got a reading of some big iron wreck about a quarter of a mile away. We headed to it. Turned out it was the *Bobinaro*, a freighter that sank in 1929. I had dived on it twenty years earlier on my honeymoon.

To give us a point of reference, we decided to build a tower on it like the Eiffel tower, only smaller. Since the whole wreck was underwater, we had to go down with burning rods and burn holes through the hull, bolt on angle iron, and weld a framework until we constructed this steel tower that stuck up out of water. We sat a man up there with our navigation equipment and a radio station. Then we started our search patterns and this system worked very well.

Next, we bought a huge tugboat, took it out there, and sank it in shallow water on a sandbar where it would stick out and we could set up another navigation and radio set. Then we started building these towers like pyramids with a small platform on top for a man and his equipment. After that it was just endless searching.

Nothing in this business happens all at once. It is very time-consuming. Thousands of man hours are involved. For instance, we searched more than one hundred thousand miles of ocean. We're still searching. We never stop. We get a reading on the mag and we dig it up to see what it is. We found airplanes, house-trailers, locomotive engines, shrimpboats, and all kinds of old and modern wrecks out there. Many times we find a wreck that is very tempting because we see dollar signs flashing down there—piles of brass or lead—but we don't have time to do much more than look at it.

One morning I had checked out about eight different magnetic anomalies. I was on the *Virgalona*, and the mag was on the *Holly's Folly*. Every time he'd get a reading, he'd drop a buoy and I would check it out. I found a buried fifty gallon drum, then some metal fish traps on another site, then I got a big pipe twenty-one feet long and a foot in diameter. At another anomaly I checked out what was probably a meteorite, but I couldn't get it. It was a big reading but it was obviously about a hundred feet down. We found probably several hundred meteorites out there.

Finally, however, I dug a hole at an anomaly and found one lead ball . . . just one round lead musket ball. I was so used to finding modern things that this really turned me on. I came up and said, "This is it!" It was in such shallow water—only twenty-two feet—that I figured it was the *Margarita*, which we knew from the records was in eighteen feet of water. This was close. Another four inches down I found a half dozen lead balls. Dug a little deeper with the duster and got a sword, also an arquebus and a galleon anchor.

At this point we had an exploration contract with the state but not a salvage contract. So we left everything there and did not bring it up. The state archaeologist came down, looked at the site, picked up all the swords and guns and took them up to Tallahassee as evidence that we had found a wreck. Then we applied for a salvage contract.

During the six months that it took to negotiate this, we were still out there searching under our exploration contract. All of a sudden we found gold—a gold chain and some coins dated 1619. I just couldn't leave that stuff there, you know [laughing]. So I brought it in, even though I did not have a salvage contract. I put it in the bank and called up the senator* and told him to come on

* Ex-Senator Robert Williams, director of the Division of Archives, History and Records Management, overseeing Florida's treasure salvage program.

down . . . that we had found something. When we finally got our salvage contract we went ahead and started digging, but there wasn't anything fast about it. We worked that whole summer and found two small gold bars and a few more coins and that was about it.

Did you find this material over a wide area rather than associated with one particular wreck?

It's all from the same wreck, but it's scattered over a large area probably half a mile long.

Did you figure this was from the Margarita?

Yes. So then we applied for a lease for three miles to the east for the *Atocha*, because by that time it was well known that the *Atocha* was one league to the east of the *Margarita*. A couple months after I applied, someone else applied for the same strip. The state turned me down and let him have it. I couldn't believe it. So I got my attorneys squawking and they kind of shelved it for about nine months, and during that time we started hauling in millions of dollars worth of stuff from the wreck—thousands of coins and all kinds of beautiful things. My son Kim made a special trip in one day with a golden chalice very ornately carved with two golden dragons for handles . . .

From the Margarita?

Well, we thought it was. But as it turned out this was from the *Atocha*. We did not know it at the time. We were convinced that it was the *Margarita* because of the depth of the water. Anyway this golden chalice has three big emeralds on the inside and studs for more. Something rattling in there is probably also emeralds. The chalice is squashed and you can't see all the way into. it. The same day, Kim brought in a large gold disk about seven or eight pounds marked with all the seals, and a golden horseshoe. We started getting lots of wonderful things—an astrolabe used to navigate in those days . . .

Was this under sand?

Yes, a tremendous amount of sand. The previous years we had worked with the *Virgalona* and there was so much sand and clay that we did not have enough horsepower to get through it all. It would take us all day to dig a hole.

In Key West the offices of Treasure Salvors, Inc., are aboard a life-size replica of a Spanish galleon named the **Golden Doubloon.** *The vessel is also a floating treasure museum where the public can view some of the treasure recovered by Mel Fisher and his divers.*

What were you using on the Virgalona?

We had two 671 diesel engines as power and two mailboxes. So I acquired two tugboats in New Orleans, brought them down to Key West, and designed two different types of dusters, one that would work on an angle with the current (there is a very strong current there), and one that would dust straight down. By using these huge digging machines we were successful in getting through all of this sand and producing about a million dollars worth of stuff a month for about five months last year.

Was it during this period that you found the silver bars?

Yes, it was last summer. My youngest son, Cain Fisher, brought the first one up. He's fifteen years old. He had been getting quite a bit of razzing from his older brothers who had each brought in millions of dollars worth of stuff and Cain hadn't found anything, so to speak. But all of sudden he was walking tall because he found a sixty-five-pound silver bar with those long complicated serial numbers, mining numbers, and assay numbers on it. The other guys brought two more of those bars in that day plus a beautiful rosary. Instead of beads, this rosary has jewels, gold balls, and a gold crucifix. There were a lot of other things. So Gene Lyon, our historian, got out the manifest of the *Margarita* to try to establish that these bars were from that ship. It took him about ten days to go through those documents because they are hand-written in archaic Spanish. And he could not find them anywhere.

So I said, "Well, try the manifest of the *Atocha*." A couple days later he came back all excited; he had found out that one of the bars was on the *Atocha* manifest. When he checked the other two, they were on the same manifest. Then we began to realize that we were working the *Atocha* and not the *Margarita*.

We had suspected this earlier before we found the bars because of the other cargo. Everything we found out there seemed to say it was the *Atocha*. Gene had kept telling me this. He said he didn't think it could be, but judging from the things we were finding, they were all listed on the *Atocha*. So, when they brought in the bars, Gene had already figured out from the manifest how much they were going to weigh. He set the scale at that weight.

They put on the bar and it balanced exactly where he had it set.

The newspapers and television got hold of it. We hired a clipping service and found that they had written twenty-six thousand articles about us. Many of them were full page spreads. Lots of newsreel guys were swarming around asking millions of questions. Also, about that time the Securities and Exchange Commission came and knocked on our door and said, "Hey, we want to check out all your papers and documents." My attorney advised me not to sell any securities or stocks and not to take in any more partners for six months until we made sure everything was okay with the S.E.C. So we did that, and about a month ago we finally got all that squared away and everything is back to normal with the S.E.C.

The silver bars then were definitely on the Atocha *manifest?*

Yes, absolutely. Everything matched. Every serial number on all three bars, every assay and *ley* mark matched precisely with those on the *Atocha* manifest.

When you got the bars up, of course they were encrusted. Did you send them up to the lab in Tallahassee to have them cleaned so that you could read the markings?

No. We could read them when we found them.

Is that right? No encrustations on them?

Yes, but they put them in a fiberglass tank that we had submerged in water. They were so heavy that when they put them in there the encrustations just flaked off. And we could read them. We had to pick up the bars about six times to look at them . . . take pictures of them and stuff.

And drop them again, eh?

[Laughing] So we could read it all just beautiful.

Where are the bars now?

In Tallahassee in the old jail at the lab.

Are all the valuable items that you recovered from that wreck site up there now in Tallahassee?

No, the last couple of loads that we brought in we still have in the bank here.

When are you going to throw it back into the ocean?

Oh . . . ahhh, that's kind of a far out thing. I'd never throw anything back in. I'd rather give it all to the state.

Then you've not reached the point that Tom Gurr did?

No. Heck, this stuff is too valuable to history to throw back in.

Were the bars the last big find that you got from that site?

Oh no, we've brought in stuff every week since then all year.

I see. What were they, silver?

All kinds. Gold and silver, jewels and coins and . . .

All dated?

. . . guns and swords and daggers, all kinds of things. We brought in a steady stream of stuff up until December fifteenth and we shut down for the holidays for a month, like we do every year. I figure the two weeks between Christmas and New Year's we never get anything done anyway. So we just all take our vacations at the same time then. About January we concentrate on rebuilding all the boats and engines and getting ready for the summer season . . . although we do have two boats working right now setting out buoy patterns and doing more detecting.

What more do you expect to do on the Atocha?

Well, we believe the main body of the wreck is in deeper water a little outside of where we are and the part we worked is part of the superstructure that broke off and drifted in. So that's where they are magging right now, to see if they can find the main pile of the wreck, which I do not believe we have gotten into yet.

You will just be expanding your search patterns then?

Yes, that's true. So far we have worked about a half a mile of the area, and the farther we go the more we find and just a little farther should be the main pile.

Do you firmly believe that this is the Atocha?

Oh yeah, we're convinced. Not only the bars, but about fifty other things indicate that. As soon as I found out from this stuff that it was the *Atocha*, I applied for a contract in the opposite direction, three miles to the west of the *Margarita* and I got that area. Now I'm sure we have both the *Atocha* and the *Margarita*. I believe we found the *Margarita* about two and a half years ago but it was right on the edge of our search area—in fact, it might have been just a hair outside of our search area but we caught it on our turns. I was afraid to dig there for fear that they would accuse me of digging outside of my search area. A couple years ago I applied for that area but they turned me down and said I had too many contracts already, and I could not have another one. But the state promised that they would not give it to anybody else. So I finally got it last November. It was approved. I haven't got it yet. They are awfully slow . . .

Would you like to add anything to all this—any advice to treasure hunters who might want to follow the same pattern that you did? Whether to stay out of it or to get into it.

Well, it's a pretty tough business. It really is. I don't want to make them think it is easy, because it takes one helluva lot of working capital and a helluva lot of perseverance and a lot of good people—a lot of good brains, men and women. It's not simple. I don't think a guy with a small crew could do it. We've got forty people now and we use all, a lot of brilliant, highly educated and talented people in the fields of history, archaeology, electronics, radioactivity, engineering, mechanics, and on and on—a lot of talent.

The ocean is awful big and awful powerful, and it destroys ships and men and equipment that costs a lot of money. It is very difficult. If they are going into it, they've got to have a million dollar budget and really go at it. Even that is tough. Once you find it, it's very difficult to sell. It takes a long time to sell treasure. You don't have a ready market. The market is improving, however. Since gold and silver have gone up, artifacts have also gone up. I'm beginning to make some good sales now, so maybe I'll catch up. But I'm still behind on the financing.

How important are stockholders to an operation such as yours?

Well, if you don't have all the money you need in the first place, the stockholders get together and each one chips in, and they each get their share of the treasure. For that reason they are extremely important. They help finance the thing. Some of them help by working, some by putting in money. They are all a part of it. We plan to work sites all over the world. It looks like we got a mighty big future because there is plenty of it out there. According to history it is there; it's not a fairy tale, and there is no doubt that these vast fortunes are there, but it's pretty tough finding them.

What areas outside our country are better set up politically and every way for treasure hunters to operate?

Bermuda has a good setup. They allow you to go out treasure hunting—just so you do not go where someone else has a contract on a wreck. That's the way it used to be here. But now they have so many rules and restrictions that it is almost impossible to operate.

Do you feel that you will eventually be squeezed out of operation by the state taking over and trying to do it?

I don't think they ever would. They could never make it succeed. In my opinion it is not something that could be run by the Russian system, where the government goes out and tries to treasure hunt.

Of course you know that Texas is doing it and keeping the private individuals out.

Yeah, Texas tried that, but it's failing. And they've approached me to come and work there. They can't do it. It's just a lot of money down the drain. The people they hired don't have the incentive, the will; they don't have that feeling of the hunt. They are not going to get rewarded, even if they do find it. It's just another paycheck. We go through all kinds of hell out in that rough ocean—storms and even annual hurricanes. We're risking our lives and doing a lot of dangerous things. State officials would not do that. They would not watch the dollars like we do either. They would blow it. I don't think they would ever succeed.

If you had it to do all over again, would you do it the same way, Mel?

Probably would. You know the state has got a real good deal the way it is. I mean, after all, what they are interested in is not treasure, they are interested in the history and the archaeology. Their only expense is paying for one state agent and operating their offices at home. Where instead of the state having to invest, say, two million dollars to do what we've done on the *Atocha*, they haven't had to invest anything and they get one-fourth of the gross of everything. It's not figured like income taxes, where you take off your expenses first and then pay your tax; they figure from the gross. And that's pretty rough when you take twenty-five percent off the top of a business. In most cases where businesses are leased out, the owner gets five or ten percent, and in this case they are getting twenty-five percent. It's a very good deal for the state. They get millions of dollars worth of gold and silver and jewels plus billions of dollars worth of historical artifacts at relatively small expense.

Yes, it would seem so. One last question, Mel. How tall are you?

Five feet, fourteen and a half inches.

In 1975, with the United States Supreme Court's clarification of state territorial boundaries off the Atlantic and Gulf coasts, Florida lost jurisdiction of the wreck site (believed to be the *Atocha*) off Marquesas Key. Subsequently, the federal government claimed all the treasure. Treasure Salvors, Inc., filed suit and won ownership in April 1976, subject to future federal appeal.

11 ~~~

Search for the Atocha

The communications media focus their sharpest attention on the newsmakers of our society, people who have either dramatically failed or dramatically succeeded in endeavors of interest to all of us. Likewise, when the media zero in on treasure hunters, they single out the newsworthy principal characters. What most of us forget is that behind every newsmaker are "contributors," people who seldom share the limelight but who have played major supportive roles in creating the success or failure of the central figure or newsmaker.

Such are the people behind treasure hunter Mel Fisher. Through the years, Fisher has worked with a small army of transients, mostly young divers who were more turned on by thoughts of what they were doing than by the jingle of coins in their jeans, unless, of course, those coins happened to be pieces of eight re-

186

ceived sometimes as wages in lieu of more negotiable lucre. But the main team, the backbone of the Treasure Salvors Company, consists of some forty staunch supporters of the Fisher dream, many of whom were with him from the very beginning, from the 360 days of no returns in 1963 through the roller coaster years of bad lows and super highs that followed. Not only are they caught up in the persistent dream, but they all share in unfaltering allegiance to their leader, Mel Fisher, the one man who by hook or crook, by Midas touch or blind luck, has held it all together and is gradually turning the dream into reality.

The interview that follows was made with two such individuals: Treasure Salvors' vice president and member of the board Bleth McHaley and company photographer and diver Don Kincaid.

Originally from Minnesota, McHaley hails from an Air Force family that lived in many places but primarily in California. She knew the Fishers when they had a dive shop business there. Coming from a background in advertising, television, and public relations, McHaley met them again years later in Key West and joined the team.

"I couldn't imagine what I would ever do for a treasure hunting company," she said. "First thing I did was run the supply boat back and forth with another guy, and then it just evolved. Everybody in this company does everything."

Twenty-eight-year-old Don Kincaid came from a background similar to McHaley's. Born into a military family in Maryland, Kincaid has lived five and a half years in Europe, several years in the Orient, and all over the United States and Mexico. He has a background in advertising and illustrative photography. Kincaid was an army photographer for three years, and after the service he became a freelance photographer working on assignments from various national publications.

In 1971 he came to Key West to do a story on Mel Fisher and ended up joining the treasure hunting company. Two days after starting work with the firm, Kincaid went out to photograph the wreck site and found an eight-and-a-half-foot-long gold money chain valued today at a quarter of a million dollars.

I interviewed Bleth McHaley and Don Kincaid in the same back room of Danny's Ice Cream Bar near the wharf and Treasure Salvors' Treasure Galleon Museum in Key West. For simplicity's sake, and to avoid the playwright's method of prefacing each bit of dialogue with the speaker's name, I have taken the liberty of not identifying which individual has made the response, since in most cases it is apparent.

Bleth, you and Don have seen both sides of this treasure hunting thing, the offshore work as well as the behind the scenes business ashore. Have you found that hunting the Atocha *so far from your home base has created special problems?*

Yes, definitely it has. Even our boats are different. All of them have two props. It's a safety precaution. Mel won't even buy a boat that has a single engine on it. It does not make any sense working out as far as we do at sea. If we were three or four miles offshore, then we could get away with one screw.

The other guys that are up the Keys really have it very easy because the stuff is so close in. Our supply lines are not just forty miles long, because you've not just got to be able to get out there but back again, too. That's eighty miles—a long distance, a lot of running time.

People ask us why it has taken so long to salvage the *Atocha*. That is one of the reasons. There isn't another treasure hunter in the state of Florida that has ever worked more than just barely out of sight of the shoreline. And here we are working forty miles out at sea. It causes tremendous problems. And in an area that no other treasure hunter has ever had to be tested on before. No other treasure hunter has had to work through twenty-five feet of sand on a shifting sandbar.

It's called the Quicksands, and with very good reason. Just within a couple miles of that wreck site there are at least two dozen wrecks out there. Sixteenth, seventeenth, eighteenth century—all the way up to modern times. There are airplanes out there, submarines, mine fields, torpedoes; we found a flatbed truck, fifty miles out at sea. A marine junkyard for the last three hundred and fifty years.

Photographer Don Kincaid and Bleth McHaley are two of Treasure Salvors most dedicated people. In an on-again off-again profession where financial rewards are sometimes long in coming and set-backs and frustrations are daily occurrences, they remain faithful to the Fisher dream.

When you stop work for a weekend or for, say, a repair period, does this cover back up again with sand, Don?

Yes. Within twenty minutes you get a four-inch layer of sand over the area, and then it fills in gradually after that at a slower rate. The bulk of it is in the first couple of minutes, and then it builds up more slowly. Overnight you'll get eight or nine inches; in a couple of days, a couple of feet.

It must be quite a job for your excavating devices, the mailboxes or dusters. Could you tell us about them and how they were used to uncover the silver bars?

Yes, it was on the *Southwind* and they were digging with the deflector rather than the dusters. There's two different techniques involved, although both use the ship's prop wash directed at the bottom. The *Northwind* and the *Virgalona*, for instance, blow straight down with the dusters and actually make a crater in the bottom through the elbow-shaped pipe. The deflectors blow at an angle and take off four-inch layers of sand at a time. They will uncover a larger area at a shallower depth, so you just take off a layer, the divers look, you take off another layer, and again they look. They deflect the prop wash at about a forty-five degree angle, whereas the other simply points it straight down so it washes a hole in the bottom. It's like using a garden hose. If you want to gently wash away some sand, you don't point it straight down; you blow it away at an angle. That's the principle involved. It is successive delayering. On this particular day we had gotten down to bedrock and had found some coins, a rosary, and a beautiful black amethyst pendant with the golden fleece on it. Really beautiful . . .

The ship stays in one place?

Yes, it's anchored. The *Northwind* and the *Southwind* both use three anchors off the stern and two off the bow. The *Virgalona* uses one in the bow and two in the stern. They have to maintain exact position. If you just hung on your bow anchor alone and turned on the engines, of course the boat would continue to swing around and wouldn't do any good at all. They have to maintain exact position. We use three- and four- and as much as a seven-point anchoring system.

How long does it take to get down through eighteen feet of sand with that setup?

Well, the thing to remember is that we don't do it all at once. We do it in little fifteen and twenty second gusts at a time that take away an inch or two, four inches, five inches, like that. And it may take all day to get down. If we did it all at once it would take a half hour or forty-five minutes, depending upon the consistency of the sand.

Do the divers move off to one side when they use it?

The advantage with the deflectors is that you can see the wash; it has little bubbles in it from the cavitation of the propellers. You can actually see the column of clear water. The divers float just above it and can see things being uncovered. As something is uncovered the diver ducks in, grabs it, and gets blown right back up again. They use it like an elevator. If you want to get down quickly you drop off the end of the deflectors, and the wash picks you up and shoots you right down to the bottom. When you want to come up, you get into it where the wash hits the bottom and it will bounce you back to the surface. It's a circular motion.

When did they start using the deflector method?

August 1972.

So this was how the silver bars were uncovered. How deep were they?

Total depth below the water surface, about thirty-eight or forty feet. At that point they were under eighteen feet of sand. It was one of the deeper sand areas.

All this occurred on the fourth of July 1973. Incidentally, in Mexico there is a shrine to Our Lady of *Atocha,* and the fourth of July is the day when they have most of their miracles. Coincidences are strong in this.

I realize that you have received a lot of criticism about these bars. From various sources I have heard that the bars actually came from the Maravilla; *they came up cleaned; they are counterfeit; the state will not declare that they are indeed from the* Atocha; *you cleaned the bars; and Mel said the encrustations were knocked off the bar by dropping it several times in the tank of water where it was being kept. What is the truth? Don, could you describe how the bars were lying when found and what you saw?*

One of the bars lay with its face (where the markings were) flat against the bedrock bottom, which is limestone, a surface of the old Florida reef. Another lay next to it with its face about an inch away from the side of the other bar. The third bar lay face up. This is the one we had to clean. Bleth and I and the state agent cleaned it with muriatic acid in front of fifty million people watching television.

He had permission to allow this?

Yes, just so Gene Lyon could check the markings. He wrote them down, did sketches of them, and then he spent five days checking them out against the manifests. The bars that did not have to be cleaned were not heavily encrusted. A mass of silver does not corrode as would an individual coin—a light knock and the corrosion and sand just dropped off. That's all there was to it.

One thing you have to understand about Mel's statements, after being a treasure hunter in the state of Florida for as many years as he has and gotten so much flak from the state, any tiny little infraction—and I mean tiny—anything he says will be very protective. In other words, he's saying, "We didn't clean those bars," because he feels that it's a defensive thing on his part. He was not entirely aware that we were allowed to clean coins and things out there, because in the past we had been told not to, that if we cleaned anything he would lose it all. But it's important that we get the information off any of the material immediately, because once it goes to Tallahassee, that's the end of it for four or five years. The entire burden of the identification of the *Atocha*, and as far as I'm concerned, all the archaeological and research work, is on Treasure Salvors because the state has never done any and I don't see them starting.

What kind of pandemonium was there when the bars came in, Bleth?

It was unbelievable. The boat radioed that they would be in by three o'clock that afternoon. The Miami *Herald* had called and I was on the phone with them when Gene Lyon walked in. We hadn't seen him for five days. He'd been at the library using their microfilm viewer every day from the time they opened until they closed, going through the entire *Margarita* manifest, and there was nothing to match the numbers and information he got from us by radio when we examined the bars at the site. So he started in on the *Atocha* manifest.

When he came in and I looked up and he said, "Where's Mel?" And I said, "He's out of town, Gene."

Then it dawned on me. I said, "What are you doing here? It's eleven o'clock in the morning." I said, "Do you have one of the bars?" And he just broke into this big grin and said, "Yes, I got one of the bars on the *Atocha* manifest."

I hung up the phone and we talked about it. Gene said, "Everything checks out on the bar, but there is one thing that we have to know and we cannot make any judgment until we know this. And that's the weight of the bar." He had the weight in marks [a former European unit of weight especially for gold and silver].

All we had on the galleon was a bathroom scale, and we decided for something as monumental as this we really couldn't weigh it on a bathroom scale. So we searched around and found a big heavy scale at the fish house of Sea Farms across the dock. We borrowed it and set it up on the deck.

In the next two hours while we waited for the boat to arrive, they converted Spanish marks to troy ounces and came up with the figure sixty-three pounds. That's what the bar had to weigh. So we preset the scale to sixty-three pounds and waited for the boat. It finally arrived at three o'clock in the afternoon, and you would have had to be there to understand the excitement and the tension. I think that's why I get so furious when people say, "It was engineered. It's all just a plot to raise money," because anybody who had been around at that time and saw this whole company with a case of the jitters couldn't possibly have believed that it was all put on.

Well, they offloaded everything from the boat before the silver bars. The National Geographic crew was on deck. They had to get set up, and there was a young newspaper reporter from the *Key West Citizen,* and the deck was absolutely jammed with people. If you are going to engineer something you don't do it out in front of God and everybody with the National Geographic photographers and the Miami *Herald* photographers, et cetera. It's done very much in secret.

So finally the bars came off, and then came the moment to weigh it . . . I couldn't look. I don't think anybody was breathing on the *Galleon.* We were watching that bar being weighed and Preston shouted, "Put it down on the scale!" and I couldn't look. I had my back turned. It was just like this; I couldn't breathe.

Then the shout went up. I turned around and the balance bar came up and didn't even waver. It just stopped right at sixty-three pounds on the nose!

That started it. There was absolute pandemonium on the

deck—everyone jumping up and down, hugging and kissing each other, and Gene Lyon is walking around with this big grin on his face, the regular quiet Gene Lyon but he's grinning. And typical of Treasure Salvors, it should have been a champagne party, but we couldn't afford champagne so we had a garbage can full of beer. That's what we were celebrating with.

It was another ten days before Gene located the other bar on the manifest. He had to leave, he was working on his dissertation and was due to go up and do his defense for his Ph.D., so he really had a lot to do. He was going through the rest of the manifest in time off from his other work. He called and said he had found the second bar. Then, about a week later he found the third one.

Was he going by numbers? What was he basing it on?

He was basing it on the bar number, the fineness or *ley* number, and the weight.

In other words, all of these had to match with the manifest data for those bars?

That's right. What our competition said is true. There can be duplications of the numbers. However, there are three sets of numbers on the bars. Chances are that on three bars that have three sets of different numbers, all checking out all three ways three times, plus one with the owner's initials on it, plus the one with the Ariola family's initials on it, plus the history of the bar is recorded—checking all those times is really beyond the realm of coincidence. I could see it happening once but not three times.

Gene made the statement, "Loaded together, [all three were loaded at Cartagena], lost together, and found together." What gripes us is that people who are not knowledgeable are making statements that are simply opinions. People get hold of a translation of the manifest, and they make broad sweeping statements based on this translation that are simply opinions rather than facts. Something is always lost in a translation. It does not include marks that are in the margin, nor does it include little writings and scribblings that are very pertinent to the information in the main body of the text. Gene said you not only have to be able to read the original, but you have to interpret what you are reading. I doubt if there is any researcher in the treasure hunting business that is more qualified than Gene Lyon.

I don't believe I will ever be fantastically rich doing this, but I would simply like to find a substantial amount of that stuff just to shut up the competition, if for no better reason.

I have already set up a procedure with Senator Williams for when the bars come out, because we got to thinking about the logistics involved. For example, there are eight hundred and ninety-eight silver bars still out there. If we came across two hundred bars, what in the world would we do with them when we got them into Key West? We couldn't put them on the *Galleon*; it would sink. The bank here wouldn't take them. They won't take the coins we found and they are considerably lighter in weight than the bars. So we have a procedure set up directly with Tallahassee, and when they come up there will be no circus; we'll get them up there first and make the announcement later.

But then, of course, you can't keep the secret. Last year we had an elaborate code set up so that it would not go out over the radio if we found a large amount of treasure. First thing that happened when we were working on the English wreck, one of the fellows got on the radio and said, "Hey, man, I got silver plates!" And Mel is the worst for that. He'll get on the radio and say, "Oh, we've got gold and silver . . ."

How many coins have come off the Atocha *so far, Don?*

Seven thousand silver and a handful of gold coins, which we did not expect to find at all. Gold coins were not minted in the New World at that time. These were Old World coins . . . in other words, someone's pocket change. There were seventy pesos in gold coins minted at Santa Fe de Bogota in 1621. And the mint master was on this fleet. We have Santa Fe de Bogota silver coins that are the very first issue of the mint. They opened the mint for a very short time, so we are hoping to come across some of those seventy pesos of Santa Fe de Bogota gold coins. Can you imagine the value? They will be more valuable than the Royals* from the 1715 fleet . . . the very first issue of the mint, only seventy pesos worth. That's it, in the whole world. I doubt if we'll find seventy of them. We might find half of them.

---

* Perfectly struck round gold coins valued at several thousand dollars apiece due to their fineness and rarity.

And one thing we have done on these silver coins is to firmly establish once and for all when the Santa fe de Bogota mint opened. That has been a controversy in the numismatic world for many years, because for one thing, nobody went to Spain to do deep research that would be necessary to establish it. But we have proved that it opened and operated for three months in 1621. We have the records and the coins to go with them.

Another thing that is interesting is that all the coin books on Potosi coins and the ones we are finding from Nuevo Reino [Colombia], which is Santa Fe de Bogota, they all claim that no coins were actually dated prior to 1617 simply because they did not know about them. They had not been found. So we've got 1611, 1612, 1601 on up. And this just blows numismatists' minds.

The other interesting thing—you look it up—in the coin catalog, the compendium, the one we use most, has a rating system for rarity. A triple "r" means one only known to exist; a double "r" is one to five known to exist; a single "r" is five to ten; an "e," which means extremely rare, less than two dozen known to exist; and sixty or seventy percent of those we have cleaned have been triple "r" 's, double rare, single rare, "e"—all those. The book gives current prices that are now ten years old. What would you give for these? Two thousand dollars apiece? Five thousand dollars apiece? Well, if you've got one that is a super rare mint mark, which we have, that's got a date that was previously unknown to exist, which we've got, plus you've got a dozen of them when there was only one known to exist. Wow! The value skyrockets!

I understand that your divisions with the state have been slow in coming due to such things as lack of conservators at the facility in Tallahassee and a generally slowed down program. That being the case, then what supports your treasure salvage operation, Bleth?

Fortunately, Mel Fisher found an awful lot of treasure on the 1715 fleet. That basically supports our operation. We get loans against it. We use it for collateral for money coming into the company. We've got left approximately two million dollars, and that is going to have to keep us going to the end of this expedition.

What has really been supporting us as far as loans go is the gorgeous gold coin collection that Mel and the company own. It is the largest and finest intact gold coin collection outside of the state of Florida. We just had an appraisal on it and the appraiser went crazy. He is an expert on precolonial coins and he had never seen such a collection. What we have is a whole bunch of dated one- and two-escudo coins, which almost don't exist outside of our hands.

Could you give me the appraised value of that collection?

The whole collection, including the gold collection, the silver collection, and the museum collection, which includes jewelry and artifacts, was appraised two weeks ago at one million nine hundred and sixty-three thousand dollars. We have another appraisal which was two million twenty-four thousand, so that is fairly close. The million nine appraisal was done by Dr. George Vote from Colonial Coins in Houston, Texas.

And I suppose stock sales make up for . . .

There are no stock sales these days. We stopped selling stock as of the fourth of July 1973.

Would you care to discuss that situation, Bleth?

We're not the only company that has been investigated by the Securities and Exchange Commission; this was a result of the publicity. No specific allegations were made by the SEC other than that we might possibly have violated Section Five of the so and so. We signed an injunction neither admitting nor denying guilt. This was to avoid lengthy litigation. The SEC did not want to go to court and we did not want to go to court, so this was the best way to do it. If we had gone to court, maybe we'd have come out free and clear as a bird. But that is a very expensive proposition that we did not want to go through. They simply said that Mel shouldn't send anything through the mail. We cannot even send a stock certificate through the mail.

There is no way that any one person can know all the SEC rules and regulations. It is very complex. The attorney told Mel there are six men in the United States that are experts on the SEC, and they are all in Washington, D.C. So we hired this individual on the advice of our local attorney and he did a good job for us. I think that when the SEC came down here and started their investigation they expected to find a man with a rowboat selling stocks to little old ladies who were mortgaging their houses. But this is what they did not find. They thought that the majority of our investors must be unsophisticated. Our major investors are people like Be Bold Products, who make bank safes throughout the world, Judge Chalmers of the Allis Chalmers Company, and some really big, major sophisticated investors. So they did not find what they expected to find. They found a going, viable operation with lots of equipment and corporate assets. Nothing really came of it.

Mel has not gotten rich from this. I don't think there are any rich treasure hunters. He borrows money from me! Absolutely true! One time I left my coin purse on the desk and went back to pick it up the next day. Don and I were going someplace in the car and stopped at a gas station. We filled the car up, I opened my coin purse to pay for it, and there was a note that said, "I owe you eighty dollars—Mel." He left me ten dollars, thank goodness. He was going out of town to raise some funds, I guess, and he didn't. have any money and my coin purse was there. He knew it was mine and he knew I really wouldn't mind. I was floored. It was the funniest thing I've ever heard of. I'll never let him live it down.

Somewhere up the line I heard some remarks about Mel being very flamboyant with some of the treasure he has found, or the wealth he has made from it. Someone said something about a solid gold briefcase or a Cadillac. Could you comment on that?

He has a gold-colored Cadillac, and as for his solid gold briefcase, he wrenched his shoulder carrying it one time. He carries treasure around with him. It's a regular briefcase, but he usually has gold bars, gold coins, one thing or another in there. We were trying to arrange some money in New York based on a whole collection of coins so we had to drag all this stuff up there. Mel had it all in his car! Now it's worth a million nine, but last year it was a million and a half. He had it in the trunk of his car and it absolutely ruined the shock absorbers.

Was this the Cadillac, Don?

No, this was the Polara. I drove him up to Islamorada to see Tom Gurr, who had a nuclear sub-bottom profiler with a range of fifteen inches, and the car was riding kind of funny but I didn't think too much about it. Then, I went to put on the brakes real hard for something and the tail-end began to swing around. Hey! What's going on! It was really riding heavy. We never quite figured it out until we got up there and they started talking treasure and Tom's crew members were all around. Pretty soon Mel says, "Hey, you guys want to see something?" And he opens up the trunk of the car and there are silver discs, gold bars, gold jewelry, and gold coins, and the rear end of the car was bottomed out back there there was so much stuff in it. And that's what the trouble was. Getting ready for that trip up there, he was carrying it around in the trunk of his car.

He left his briefcase in the backseat of a taxi cab recently. Of course the cab driver got it. They all know who Mel is, but they opened it up and there were the gold bars, gold discs, and coins. They were going to spirit it away; they had already divided it up and figured they were rich for life. They were saying, "What are we going to do with this? How do we sell it?" And Mel walked in and said, "Gee, I'd kinda like to have my briefcase back, you guys." And they said, "Oh, okay." And Mel gave them each a piece of four* . . . for stealing his briefcase! Can you imagine?

Mel doesn't have a nickel, he really doesn't. He's put all of his own money back into the company. The corporation owes him personally so much money. He hasn't collected a paycheck in God knows how long—just flat expenses, because if we're running short of money he doesn't take a paycheck. His only source of outside income is the lease on his dive shop in California, which he never sold when he came to Florida. So he gets "X" number of dollars every month, which is just a pittance—that's all, about four hundred dollars. He is not a rich man. But he does like to carry treasure around with him. And that's where he gets the reputation of being flamboyant, I think. You never find him without a gold bar or something in his pockets.

Is it real stuff or simply a copy?

No, no, this is the stuff from the 1715s. We have some repro-

---

* A colonial period Spanish silver coin of four reals.

ductions of coins on the *Galleon*, but we're getting rid of those because we want to have nothing but real stuff there. We don't sell any reproductions of coins on the *Galleon*. On the tour we make no bones about it and tell people that the coins they see below are real. We try to explain to them why some of the things they see will be reproductions rather than the real thing. The reason, of course, is the value. We have a six thousand dollar reproduction of the Rio Mar cross on display instead of the original, which is worth eighty-five thousand dollars. Because there is no way that we are going to hang an eighty-five thousand dollar cross down there. They did before in Fort Lauderdale and got ripped off to the tune of half a million dollars.

When was that?

When they were at Pier Sixty-six, thieves broke into the *Galleon*, held the guard at gunpoint, and ripped it off. We got most of it back. They left a trail of silver coins. This guy was running across the parking lot carrying a seventy-pound cluster of silver coins. He got caught because he wouldn't drop it.

Ahhh, the classic ending.

And when the big news hit last year, it was hysterical. This town filled up with people, including continental jewel thieves, robbers, *et cetera*. Two guys were arrested . . . they went to the yacht club and tried to charter a boat to go out to the wreck site and pick up all the gold that is lying on the bottom of the ocean. And they tried all down the boat fleet and nobody would charter to them. So they got arrested trying to steal a boat down by A and B Lobster House. They just were not aware that if they had gotten out there and did find the wreck site it would have been a great shock to them. They expected to go down and find gold laying all over the place. For crying out loud, do they honestly think we would leave a site with everything like that laying around?

Would you care to speculate on where the bulk of the Atocha *is? What has happened? Why can't you find it with the magneto-meter?*

If Mel were sitting here he'd say, "Well, I found it on the last trip." And we might have. We did a magnetometer survey less than a week ago, and I was running the mag on the boat and we did a complete survey. We have a concentration of readings, but they are under quite a bit of sand in deeper water and we were with the *Virgalona*, which does not dig in deeper water. But it's the right amount of magnetic material. Also, it is right in line with the scatter patterns from our wreck site. We know that the storm scattered things and we went right down the line and here was this concentration.

All the time that we have been out there we have dug considerably less than a third of that site. That's what people don't understand. Look how long Tom Gurr worked the *San José* and he was still finding material. So are we—not a fantastic amount, but there is still material there. You can rework a site and rework it.

Those silver bars, you say there were hundreds of them aboard the Atocha. *You don't think of them moving around much when a ship goes down. When the hull was ripped open you would think most of them would go to the bottom and stay fairly close together.*

The thing to remember—and people forget this every time—there were two storms, not just one. When the *Atocha* first struck bottom, went on a little ways and sank in deeper water with the sterncastle awash and the mizzenmast sticking out, the Spanish salvors were able to come back and find it. It was obvious, with everything sticking out of water. They sent divers down, but they couldn't get into it because it was intact. They managed to recover two cannons and, I think, a chest of coins. They had to leave because the weather was threatening. They went to the Tortugas and found the *Rosario*, unloaded all that stuff and split.

A week later another hurricane hit. When the salvors came back, they could no longer find the *Atocha*; the decks were no longer awash, the mizzenmast was not there, and they found part of the bow on the Marquesas. In other words, an intact wreck had broken at least in half, probably in more parts than that. Much of the silver and things were stored in the sterncastle, although not up in the top, but down in the bottom. The sterncastle apparently broke off; the bow apparently broke off—they found part of the bow on the beach. Most of the material that we've been recovering is from the stern section. There is a shallow bank near deeper water, and the direction of the second storm apparently broke off the sterncastle, wedged it against the sandbar, pounded it to pieces, and it fell apart right there. The bow went down into the Marquesas, where the Indians actually recovered coins from it. That other chunk of the wreck, apparently the third part, is out in deeper water which is where we got these other readings. That's the thing that people don't remember—that this thing is scattered literally from where we're working now all the way to the Marquesas, ten miles. All along the edge of that sandbar you can get magnetic readings. But they are outside our area, so we can't dig on them. On the Marquesas I have found pottery, nails, and ballast stones of the same type we have found on the wreck site. So there is definitely stuff scattered over a minimum area of a quarter by a half a mile and a maximum area of possibly ten miles.

The area where you found the bars is ten miles from the Marquesas?

Yes, roughly that. About west-southwest of the island.

And the scatter pattern seems to be in which direction?

Well, there are two scatter patterns. This is the thing you've got to remember—the first storm and the second storm. There is an initial scatter pattern, then a secondary dispersal. The secondary dispersal frankly goes in two directions.

Another thing you've got to remember is that a storm is a circular pattern; it blows in two different directions, depending upon what part the eye goes through. That is the second hurricane. We've got one basic scatter pattern that goes from deep water up to the northwest of our area, of which we have only dug about one-third; we've got another that goes out in the direction of the Marquesas where the bow was. The documents say that this part consisted of one-eighth of the forepeak with the strakes attached, which is the bulk of the bow.

Commander Clare of the U.S. Navy, a meterorologist, took the information that Gene Lyon gave him from the archives, including the weather in Havana at the time, which Gene dug up from the Havana *legajos*, all the reports from the inquiry, and so forth, and he plotted the course of the vessels, using modern technology that took into consideration ship weights, currents, drift factors, the given amount of wind which was recorded at that time, how fast a high-pooped ship would drift and in what direction under those conditions, and by applying these as applicable mathematical factors, he came up with the opinion that the first storm was not a full hurricane—that it was a severe tropical storm with the winds up to seventy-four miles an hour. He plotted the course of these vessels and, without knowing the coordinates of our wreck site, put them within one mile of where we are working. He said there is no possible way that those vessels could be anywhere than right where we think they are.

It was physically impossible for the amount of time and drift involved for them to be any place farther north of the Keys than Key West.

The fact is the *Rosario* went aground in the Dry Tortugas. Now with all the talk about the fleet going down around the Matecumbes, there is just no way that one vessel is going to ground on the Dry Tortugas two hundred and some miles away— because they were all together, within sight of each other in a fleet.

Another bit of information to knock out the Matecumbe theory, which I don't think anybody is too excited about anymore, is the fact that when the Spanish salvagers were working on the *Margarita*, the Dutch came around the north end of the island and ran them off. Well, they would have to sail in one foot of water to come around the north end of the island at the Matecumbes. It is impossible.

There is only one place in the entire Keys where you can do that, and a look at any set of navigational charts will show that it is around the Marquesas. It also says in the research, "We landed at Cayo del Marques," which is named after the Marques de Caldereita, the owner of the *Atocha* and the *Margarita* and also the director of the salvage.

As Duncan Mathewson would put it, he agrees as an archaeologist that the three silver bars alone are not enough archaeological evidence to identify it as the *Atocha*. But if you take into consideration the historic documentation, the geographic docu-

mentation, and you put all this together, there is just nothing else
that it could be.

As far as anyone saying that it could be one of the lesser
vessels of the fleet, well, there were three major vessels of the fleet
lost: the *Rosario*, the *Margarita*, and the *Atocha*. The others were
simply small pataches, small merchantmen that carried no heavy
cannon. The amount of weaponry that we have found indicates a
capital vessel. The size of the cannon, the stone cannonballs, and
the great number of cannonballs that we have found, indicates a
capital vessel. There were only two ships in the fleet that carried
stone cannonballs: the *Margarita* and the *Atocha*.

Where were the cannon found?

Over in the deeper water. They are nonmagnetic, all bronze.
There were eighteen aboard the *Atocha*. The ship was the fleet's
Almiranta. She weighed six hundred sixty tons. Her keel was only
seventy-nine feet. In other words her keel was as long as one of our
tugboats. She was roughly a third smaller than our *Galleon* but as
tall in the sterncastle. Unloaded she drew eighteen feet of water.
The height of the mast was only eighty-nine feet. That mast out
there on the *Galleon* is one hundred eighteen feet.

What's the length of the Galleon, *Don?*

One hundred and sixty-seven feet. Keel length is one hundred
and ten feet. So here was a vessel measuring a third less than our
Galleon but weighing a third more, not counting cargo. People
think of them as being huge ships with thousands of people
aboard, but they weren't. They were not much bigger than a big
shrimp boat.

Someone made the statement that it might be one of the
Spanish salvage vessels that sank at the site. Well, there is no
record anywhere in the documentation of any salvage vessel sinking out there. They lost the *frigata* at the Marquesas quite close in.
The fact is, it is impossible for it to be a salvage vessel because,
number one, they would not have salvaged their weapons, which
would have been unusable after a year or so under water. And
they did not find the *Margarita* until four years after it sank.
Number two, they wouldn't have salvaged the indigo. There is no
market for wet, soggy indigo, and in one area there is almost three

feet of indigo. Our divers were coming up stained blue. I was taking movies while the duster was going and you could see where worms had made holes and their worm tubes were lined with indigo. Here were these little wisps of indigo off like that, then you got into it more and, whoosh, instead of white sand being blown, there would be blue indigo all over the place. Indigo originally is yellow-green, but once it oxidizes it becomes a blue dye. And this has already been oxidized.

Was that cargo from Cartagena?

No, this indigo was loaded at Havana. It came in on another vessel, from Honduras along with a cargo of rosewood. The little bit of wood that has been found on the site has been the pallets that were between the bales of indigo. I wish the state would do something with that wood, because there could be some good dating. It looks new, except that it breaks very easily.

We have yet to find the main ballast pile out there, and this is where we are now concentrating our main effort. Because when they salvaged the *Margarita*, the Spanish had to move the ballast to get to the silver bars. They had nine hundred and one silver bars, each of them weighing a thousand ounces. So you figure out the weight. It amounts to many tons [actually 28.2 tons]. They would not put all that in the stern. It would have been laid on top of the ballast, all along the keel—used as ballast probably.

When we have a party aboard the *Galleon*—say we have three hundred people—the waterline goes down about a foot and a half. For a vessel a third smaller than the *Galleon*, the silver bars would weigh much more than all those people, so they had to have gone down quite a bit.

Have you checked to see where your solid bedrock is, Don?

In the Quicksands part of the wreck site, the sand varies from none at all on the edge of a slope to a depth of twenty feet of sand. In the deeper water where the *Atocha* first sank, we measured the depth to the keel we found at fifty-four feet. The depth in the area where we got the bulk of our magnetic readings is thirty-five or forty feet, so there is at least that much overburden there, if that's the wreck underneath it. We have to go on the presumption that it is.

How much overburden then?

Well, from fifty-four feet to forty feet—fifteen feet at least. In this type of bottom where we've got the main set of readings the bottom is very convoluted. There are pits, fine silt. Nothing is growing there; it is all dead. The local fishermen call it a lake in the sea because, when the water is clear every place else, the water does not move in there and it stays muddy longer.

Is this within your salvage area?

Yes.

I know that primarily this company started out interested solely in treasure hunting, but now you have become involved with the archaeological aspects and have hired a knowledgeable archaeologist to work with you. What can you tell me about that?

Our archaeologist, Duncan Mathewson, has been a real revelation. As a result of his work here he has published at least two papers. His one paper, which he gave at the archaeological conference in San Francisco, dealt with the lack of publication on what he termed shallow-water archaeology, to differentiate between archaeology of the type done in the Mediterranean by George Bass.

There are two entirely different theories involved. Some of the principles are applicable, but most are not. After three hundred and fifty years of hurricane, how much stratification are you going to find?

Duncan feels that you have to tie it in historically, not just the provenience of the artifacts you find out there, but what relation they have to the development of Florida and the United States. Our English wreck for instance. About the time it went down they were settling Mobile, and he feels that he could probably tie into Mobile or to Jamestown. It is all in the same period. And this is the direction that he is taking.

I believe that when the salvage and all the study and research is through on the *Atocha*, this will be the most well documented, well researched vessel ever worked. It is kind of a pilot program because we are the first company to really make an effort to do something more than just be the greedy treasure hunters . . . on our own behalf, not because the state said we had to do this. The state did not say, "Go out and hire an archaeological consultant." We did that on our own. And it was Mel who found Gene Lyon. It takes us out of the same class as other treasure hunters. Of course, we are larger and have more facilities.

I wonder if perhaps *treasure hunter* is still the real term any more. It is a little outmoded for us. Admittedly there certainly is interest in gold and silver and jewels, *et cetera*, but we have really gone beyond that now.

The bulk of publications on this wreck will be scholarly and academic publications. There will, of course, be popular books written about it, I am sure, but the bulk will be academic and this will be the first time that has ever been done. Gene said that he is almost in awe of the information coming out as a result of this wreck site. Of course he is a historian and his field is the Spanish in Florida. For example, as a result of his research on the *Atocha*, he has been able to come up with the original Indian names for all of the Keys, which was previously unknown. There is an enormous amount of this kind of completely new information coming out of Gene's research on these shipwrecks—important links with Florida and the history of the United States.

Speaking of links, Don, I understand that you found a few baubles out there yourself. Would you tell us about that?

Well, it happened in 1971, just after I started work with the company. It was still the quest at that point; they had not found the wreck. Up to then they had found one coin, a rifle, and a galleon anchor. A couple days after I started work I went out to the site to take some photographs underwater. I dove down and found an eight-and-a-half-foot-long gold chain now valued at a quarter of a million dollars. That throws a photographer or writer's objectivity right out the window. This is a so-called "money chain" with large links about three-eighths of an inch long. As I mentioned earlier, until then, there were no gold coins in the New World except for the seventy from the Bogota mint. So people made up these chains and each link was a specific weight. When you went to a merchant you broke off a link to pay for your purchases.

Are the links all the same weight?

Yes, all those in this particular chain are. But individuals made up chains to their own amount of change, what they could carry around easily. They just wore them around their necks or put them in their pockets, I imagine. So as a result of giving all those links to all those merchants, all these chains are disseminated and only a couple other complete ones have ever been found. I believe this is the largest intact one, which is why it is worth a quarter of a million dollars.

Are the links oval?

Yes, they are made of extruded wire. When you make wire out of gold, you put the gold through a hole—which in this case had uneven edges, so the wire came out with lines along the sides of it. They took one length of wire and left it straight. They took another length and twisted it, which is one of the things you can do with gold, and gave the wire a spiral shape. So, with every other link, one is spiraled and one is straight. The total length is eight and a half feet. It was in three pieces when I found it, all balled up on the bottom. At first I thought it was brass. I had never seen gold underwater—it looks green. But the closer I got to the surface the more it looked like gold. The only treasure I had found prior to that was an 1862 coin from a Civil War wreck.

Don, what denomination is the gold coin you are wearing around your neck?

It's a two-escudo coin made in Bogota, Colombia, according to the crest on it. There is no date on it, but I can roughly date it about 1690. The design around the mounting is the same as that on the coin. It's a royal flower motif, which is the same as the flower petal link chain recovered from the 1715 fleet. Those were olive blossoms and I presume that's what these are.

Did you find the coin?

No, it was given to me as a bonus for finding the gold chain, in addition to some cash.

Have either one of you anything that you would like to add before we wind up this interview—perhaps what your hopes are for the future?

Well, we've got a team of knowledgeable, professional, dedicated people. At this point we are all really wanting to get it done—to get it over with so that we can go on to something else, because frankly we are getting bored with the *Atocha*. The work now is simply the hard work, the drudgery, and there are other things that we want to go on to.

You know, the treasure hunt . . . the hunt is a quest. The *Atocha* has been found, not all of it, of course. But the quest part, which is usually the part that interests most people, is really at a standstill. Like Bleth said, now is the hard part: the drudgery, the actual physical recovery, the work involved. To individuals—the divers for instance—finding individual objects, that's the hunt for them. But for Mel it is no longer the same thing as when you know, "Oh, it's out there someplace . . ." It's not the same. He wants to have another quest.

Could you draw me a word picture of a typical treasure hunter, perhaps of the Mel Fisher personality? Describe for the reader what actually sums up their personality, what characteristics they have that are different from the average person.

Some may be tall, some may be short, some may be quiet, some may be voluble, but the first characteristic that all treasure hunters have is an obsession. And Mel Fisher has that obsession stronger than any other treasure hunter. He has a drive that is not restricted by imagination. There is no such thing as impossible. Treasure Salvors has found everything it has ever looked for because of Mel Fisher's drive. There is no way that we can't do a thing; we do it no matter what.

Does this obsession ever go beyond good reason?

Sure it does; it has to. If you restricted everything with reason, then you could not go on. Mel Fisher has done things that they said were impossible—things that had never been done before, that people said simply could not be done. Yet, he did them. This is what makes the difference between treasure hunters and usually the difference between success and failure.

12 $\sim\!\!\sim\!\!\sim$

EUGENE LYON: NUGGETS IN THE ARCHIVES

In fact or fiction, treasure hunters of the past habitually found their way to fame and fortune with the time-honored treasure map. One clue led to another, "X" marked the spot, finders keepers, losers weepers, and the devil take the rest.

Today things have changed. Serious treasure hunters backed by an army of stockholders, scientists, scholars, and gentlemen adventurers armed with sophisticated space-age digging and detection devices no longer rely on "ye olde authentic treasure map." Today that cherished piece of rolled parchment with the candle-smoked edges, cryptic scrawls, and coded messages has been replaced by a research historian. Not as romantic perhaps but a lot more reliable.

Dr. Eugene Lyon, forty-five, is one such individual. Gene told me that he was in his third or fourth career—he wasn't sure. Trained as a city manager, he was an assistant manager in Coral

Gables, Florida, an assistant to the first county manager in Dade County, and later went to Vero Beach as city manager, a position he held for nine years. From there he transferred over to school administration, became business manager of a college, and went back to school for his Ph.D. in history, primarily because he loved the subject and was particularly interested in Florida history.

Gene is a tall, slender, softspoken, scholarly man with black hair, modishly long sideburns, and glasses. On the March afternoon that we met, he was wearing an open-neck sport shirt and dark trousers. The interview took place in the admiral's cabin of Treasure Salvors' full-size replica of a Spanish galleon, moored beside the wharf at Key West.

Gene, seated behind a desk stacked high with thick file folders packed with photographs and documents relative to his historical research on the *Atocha,* was disturbed by a recent Miami *Herald* article disputing the company's claims to have found treasure from the *Atocha.* And not knowing what I wished to interview him about, he had come prepared to defend the company's position on the subject.

I tried to make it clear that I was more interested in finding out how one delves into centuries-old oddly written Spanish records in musty Spanish archives and comes up with the nuggets of vital information that directs treasure hunters to their targets. To begin with I asked how an academic historian like Eugene Lyon got involved in the treasure hunting business.

Florida history is not a field at the University of Florida. You are either a U.S. historian or a Latin American historian, so I picked Latin American history. I had some professors who were interested in paleography, the science of reading older script in foreign languages. While at the university I got the opportunity to go to Spain and do some work on Florida materials at the AGI [Archivo General de Indias], the General Archives of the Indies in Seville, which is the main depository for most of the papers concerning the Spanish colonial empire. I went there in 1969 for my dissertation research. When it was finished I met Mel Fisher in Seville who asked me to do some research on the *Atocha* for him.

After he returned to the United States, I found the salvage papers of the *Margarita* in the archives.

Could you tell me in detail about the first time you went to the archives? Did the school lay the groundwork for you by telling them that you were coming? Did you have special contacts? Translators?

No. They shouldn't let you go to the Archives of the Indies and try to read the material unless you not only know Spanish well, but are also able to read very peculiar script. Here, for example, is a sample, a script called *processol*, which is a notary public's script. (He shows me a Xerox copy of continuous penwriting.)

Now what is this written in?

Spanish.

But not the Spanish of today.

Yes. Very much the Spanish of today. The language is changed very little. But the script . . . the writing is different. If someone goes to the AGI as many treasure hunters do—or many dear little ladies looking for something about Christopher Columbus, or many people looking for the lost mines of something or other in Arizona or Mexico—unprepared to read these materials, they have a choice. They can either leave or they can hire a Spaniard who is trained to read the script. And there are very many fine workers there who can do this.

At what rate?

Quite reasonable. It varies. The best of them . . . they charge by piece work, usually one hundred to two hundred pesetas an hour perhaps. It is fifty-eight pesetas to a dollar now.

Where do you contact these people?

At the archives. Many of them work there. Most Americans who want Spanish material do it by correspondence. Or if they come there and find they cannot use the material, then they hire one of these people to work for them. Mel did a lot of that. A lot of the material we have—twenty or thirty thousand pages of material—comes from some very fine copyists or workers over there. It came here, and I then translated and interpreted it for his use. But it is all written manuscript material. Usually it is written in ink made from the gall of oak trees on very fine paper. Many of the things are four hundred years old. Our paper is not as good as theirs was. It was high linen content paper and it lasted. This is three hundred fifty-two years old, that registry [showing a Xerox of the original]. They will not let you take the originals out of the Archives of the Indies. They will make you microfilm or Xerox or photographic copies, whichever you want.

How do you tell someone about the ship you are researching —for example, tell someone that you want everything pertaining to the Atocha?

No. You would not find anything that way. You would probably get the same packet of information that has been sold to all the treasure hunters. And the problem of the word *Matecumbe* in this shipwreck arises because all of these people were sold the same packet of materials by the same dear good lady. And they did not go beyond it. They did not understand the geography of the Keys, the meaning of the word *Matecumbe*, or they were not able to search, or did not have their copyist search parts of the archives which gave Marquesas Key as the actual location of the shipwreck. So then we found the Cuban accounting papers for 1630, which gave us the salvage papers of the *Margarita* and our clue to the location. Then we were miles ahead of anyone else until our first rival, following closely on our heels, found the same material. But it took them two years and it was too late.

Is this the document that says something to the effect that "as I look out I see the Atocha *going down"?*

No, that's a very familiar document. The first time I saw that document it had Bob Marx's mark on it in the archives.

In the archives? What kind of mark?

Yes. They allow you to put a *ficha* or small bookmark in the document so that it can be microfilmed. When the photographic lab at the archives does the filming, they call for the *legajo* or bundle of documents, take it to the cellar, and film it. You've put in a request on paper and then they are supposed to remove the *ficha* from the file, but sometimes they don't. And they had not removed this.

So this was a break-through. The proper use of a manifest is very new in this business, and it is not well understood. It's a tremendous break-through because it means that you can positively identify a shipwreck. In the last few years a lot has appeared in newspapers and other publications about a whole number of shipwrecks found off the Florida coasts. From those wrecks found, very few have really been identified. There is, for example, a wreck over in the north end of Grand Bahama which everyone says is the *Maravilla*. Where is the identification? Do you know of any identification? I don't. There is a *San José*, 1733. What's the identification of the *San José*?

Just that it was there between the other two wrecks and had the properly dated coins.

Fine. That's good beginning evidence for a hypothesis. Identification is a hypothesis. We came up with dates on six thousand coins and stone cannonballs. We know that both the *Atocha* and the *Margarita* carried *pedreros*, which threw stone cannonballs, and each ship carried sixty stone cannonballs. We came up with cargo items—indigo and bar copper—both of which were loaded in Havana aboard the *Atocha*. We came up with bar gold and a richness of jewelry that indicates a capital shipwreck. Then we located specific items that can be found on the manifest. We've identified the ship. How many bars do we have to find before we've identified the ship, when there is no controversy about the identification of these other ships? They have not even been identified, but they are called the *Maravilla, San José, et cetera.* I'm just appealing for a little factual justice at this point.

Of course.

I am not concerned at this point with the private interest of this shipwreck [the *Atocha*]; I'm talking about research capabilities for the future. If you can really utilize the manifest, you are going to know a whole culture. Not just bar silver, not just gold pieces that are identifiable on the registry, not silverware that you can trade in a few cases (not many, because silverware is very vague in the registry). But you are talking about the whole economic, governmental, financial system of the Spanish Empire. You're talking about the marine technology and the culture that these people inherited from the Phoenecians, the Greeks, the

Romans, and the Portuguese. One of these bars, for example, number 4584, was shipped by the royal officials at Cartagena [Colombia] in payment for African slaves brought from the Guinea coast and sold at Cartagena. Upon each black man or *pieze de Indias*, one unit of slavery, (it might be three children, or two women, or one strong young man) the Crown collected a certain tax on each head. And this bar was sent back, double blood money, because it was bought with the blood of the Indians who mined it, whether it was mined in Bogotá or Potosí or wherever it was mined. And then it was paid for with the blood of the African slaves shipped back and lost in the Florida Keys. And later, that same bar served to identify a shipwreck. Fascinating.

I spent a day with Sonny Cockrell* going through the registry, and it is a marvelous document. But until you know how to read a registry, you cannot know what is in it. Until you understand the empire that stood in back of it, the officers and men who administered it, the jealousies in the fleet system and the problems

* Wilburn "Sonny" Cockrell, Florida state underwater archaeologist.

Hard-working historian and research specialist Dr. Eugene Lyon corrected a translation error and found a clue in Seville's Archives of the Indies that hurried treasure hunter Mel Fisher into the Marquesas Keys hot on the trail of the wreck of the Atocha.

between the merchants and the fleet generals, you can't talk about the cargo of a ship. You're just picking something up on the Florida beach and saying, well, here's a piece of treasure. . . . What I'm saying is that we are learning. People are learning more about coins and learning more about the construction of these ships. We've got the construction contract for the *Atocha* here. She was built on bid, which is maybe part of the reason why she sank. We hope to be able to reconstruct this ship. We are working now with our archaeologist on the English equivalent of the old Spanish terminology for parts of a vessel, trying to put them together. This isn't my field. I'm just getting my feet wet and I'm finding it fascinating.

What I'm really saying is that the whole area of research is absolutely in its infancy in this business. Nothing has been done. No shipwrecks have been found. A few shallow-water shipwrecks? The first unsalvaged wreck that is found will be a financial revelation. It will spark a revolution as big as the 1715 ships sparked in Florida. Hundreds of corporations were formed; people got excited. I know; I lived in the area when it was going on. Let the first deep wreck really be exploited—and the *Atocha* may be it— and you'll see investments, technology advances in diving and navigation systems; in archival research there will be fifty people over there like me looking. And by that time I will be doing something else. It will have lost its challenge at that point. If it gets to that, I'm not interested in the crowd.

Where did you learn to read this type of script?

I just sweated through one summer. I knew Spanish fairly well.

Were you working with someone who could tell you something about this script?

No. I had two professors at the university who gave courses in paleography and this was a real help. But when it came to *processal* and some of the other scripts, I had not had much practice. So, a colleague of mine from LSU sent back to the University of Florida eight reels of film, the accounting papers for Florida. I translated them and indexed them and sweated them out that summer and learned to read that stuff. That's all it took was a summer.

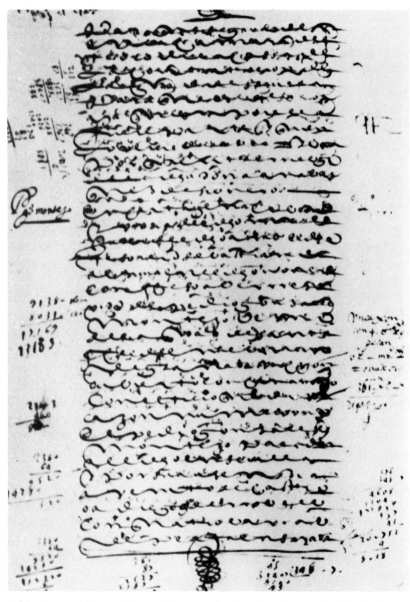

This page of the gold manifest for the Atocha *shows the kind of continuous script that research historian Eugene Lyon must translate in his search for clues that will lead to the lost treasure galleon.* (Courtesy Don Kincaid)

That's incredible.

No, it's a very mechanical skill. Someone with the knowledge of Spanish and the ability to guess what they mean in the next word can do it easily.

I speak Spanish and have lived in Spain for almost four years, where I spoke it fairly fluently. But I don't see any similarity to any of the words on that Xeroxed document.

Let me just trace through here.

What did you call this?

A *processal*; that's a notary public's script. This is a page of the registry, probably from Cartagena because those I photographed listed the three silver bars that are all in the Cartagena registry. It simply describes each bar bit by bit. *Vara de Plata.* Rather than *Bara*, they used the "V" instead of the "B".

It is all written together.

That's right. It's like a secretary with poor Gregg shorthand. You know Gregg. You've got an "R" and an "L" that look the same, but one is longer than the other. Or you've got some of the upright characters like "Y" "O", "U" and then something that would stick up higher. But in this script they do not discriminate in the height of letters.

Yes, I can see how they have done it, now that you point it out.

The words are *encadenada*; they are all enchained together. There is no punctuation, no periods, nothing. You've got to just pick out a place to stop. It's not hard. You'd be doing it in a week.

Really?

Yes. You just have to sweat it through, break through that barrier. They wrote on both sides of a folio page, and sometimes it is confusing because the ink has bled through. Originally the ink was probably black, but it has now faded to various shades of brown.

Did I understand you correctly when you said that Matecumbe was synonomous with the Florida Keys? I thought the word the Spanish used was Los Martirs, *the martyrs.*

Well, Matecumbe is synonomous with the great bulk of the

island keys below Key Largo. The entire chain is called *Los Martirs*. The *Cabeza de Martirs* is the head of the martyrs, which has been used for both the northern and the southern keys.

Then perhaps it depended upon which way you were approaching them. Could that be?

Possibly. I have been studying the history of the lower keys and find it fascinating. So what happens when a group of treasure hunters, reading the canned material that is sent to them, discover that the ships were lost in the *Cayos de Matecumbe*? And not learning that after that material which came from the papers of the Armada and other sources, the fleet commander, the Marqués de Caldereita, comes to Marquesas Key, a barracks is built there and for three months he helps direct the salvage. It takes the name, the *Cayos del Marquesas* as it shows on later maps, and on the salvage papers from 1630. But the treasure hunters did not dig that much past the immediate shipwreck.

You've got to dig for fifty years. You've got to find that when people retire—when they put their memoirs on record, trying to get attention from the crowds—that's when you get good material. Look thirty or fifty years after a shipwreck. It's hard work.

How do you know what to look for? Do you just look for anything that was published after that period?

It's a complicated and complex thing. You have to understand the archives—where the papers came from to be deposited there, how they were laid down, and where you are likely to find what you are looking for. Most people went through all the *Audencia Papers*. These are correspondence files that deal largely between the governor of some area and the king. Bob Marx found an awful lot of material in his good book on *Shipwrecks in Florida Waters* from Santo Domingo 101, which is in that series of files. But you have got to go to other papers to find more shipwreck data—for example, the accounting papers of Cuba. An odd place to look for material, but there it is. That's where we found the clue. That's this particularly worm-eaten page here. Those things were apparently stored in Cuba, maybe until 1898. I don't recall their particular history, but those we have were badly worm-eaten. Finally they ended up in Seville where they are being cared for properly now. I think probably there are more copies of this in Florida now than there were, but we got the first copy.

This, for example, is an audit, a dry-as-bones audit of the papers of the salvor. And it describes how the auditor comes in to audit this man's salvage work. And here it mentions the *Cayos del Marquesas*. This put us on the track to mount this long sea search around Marquesas. And because the copyist had erred in sending along something from one of the Santo Domingo papers—this thing you were talking about, the eye-witness report of Bernadina del Lugo—because she had erred in transliterating the word *east* to *west*, we searched east of the Marquesas for months. We finally sent for the original of the document and found that the error had been made. We hadn't been west for more than a month and a half when we found the galleon anchor that proved to be the nucleus of the shipwreck. It was the difference between the words *oueste* [west] and *veste* [east], spelled with a "v" on that document.

What do you think it might cost an individual who does not have the scholastic background but who has found a wreck to research it in the Archives of the Indies in Seville? He goes there and has to hire people to do this work for him. Now, could he get much of a search job done by paying someone to look it up for him?

Yes. An awful lot has been done on that basis. However, it seems imprecise to me. You can't point another set of eyes and another brain in the direction that you want to go. They may tend to simply give you what they have given other people. Or they may not search diligently all of the area that you want. You have no way of knowing. But a lot has been done that way.

Could you give me a general idea of what a research job of this nature would cost?

It would be hard for me to say. Some people apparently take the shotgun approach, they go to compile as complete a list of shipwrecks and dates as they can. I would take a rifle approach, looking for one particular thing. Or conversely, if you find a promising thing, you follow it up completely until you know what that ship carried and what was salvaged from it. Otherwise, you're wasting your time. Why search for it if it was completely salvaged? Why waste your efforts and your dollars?

So it depends upon your approach. And you can search for months and not find what you are looking for. That's the problem with the rifle approach. You cover an awful lot of territory to yield a small amount.

Using the rifle approach you speak of, what would you consider a reasonable expense for the research work on something like that?

It's really difficult to say. You could find something in a few months, or it might take a year. And it is just simply the cost that it takes to live there. Your cost of living is small.

Yes, I know. But I am speaking about the uninitiated, the nonscholar who has to hire his experts to try to find as best a thing as he can. Certainly somewhere back there at the very beginning, these people, these treasure hunters were not knowledgeable about these things, yet they were able to get information that helped them. Kip Wagner managed to get information relative to the 1715s. What I am trying to get at is roughly what kind of expense is it going to take—twenty thousand dollars to get a little bit of knowledge?

No, I would not think so. I don't have the faintest idea what Kip Wagner spent. I know, for example, he went to the University of Florida, where there is a lot of 1715 material in a special collection. Wagner got that material reproduced and he couldn't read it, so he took it to Luis Arana at the Castillo de San Marcos at St. Augustine and Luis read it for him.

But to answer your question, I don't know how to approach it. The field is new. A company could hire a man full-time, reward him with stock percentages or dollars or whatever, or could contract with someone, part-time or full-time. It's new. I know a couple major treasure hunters mentioned that they were going to New York to locate a researcher who could work directly in the AGI, because they found it very unsatisfactory to deal with the copyists and try to get anything out of the material. So this will probably be the trend. But the reason the cost of it is difficult to assess is because it depends upon what you are looking for: how many sites you want, how much data you want on them. At fifty-eight pesetas to a dollar, you could expect to pay a researcher about one hundred to two hundred pesetas an hour—very reasonable.

Could you give me an idea of what a researcher of your caliber could expect to earn in a year's time?

I can't really say, because as far as I'm concerned, I'm a stockholder in this corporation, I'm involved with a percentage of the finds. I get paid a salary or contract amount and other emoluments. So what it is going to add up to is what I *hope* it will add up to. It has not added up to a whole lot yet. This corporation has not been in a position to add up to much of anything.

Well, I hope it all works out well. They are certainly hard at it.

Well, if it doesn't, it has still been very interesting.

13 ~~~~~

C. DUNCAN MATHEWSON: THE SHARK CANNON

There are many who believe that underwater archaeology and
treasure hunting are totally incompatible with each other. Treasure hunters chafe at working with archaeologists because the
former claim the latter slow them down and time is money.
Archaeologists chafe at working with treasure hunters because the
former claim the latter are only intent on tearing up historical
wrecks in search of treasure. As one archaeologist so aptly put it,
"If I find a plank from a shipwreck, I may want to photograph it,
measure it, and tag it; whereas the treasure hunter only wants to
lift it up to see if there is any treasure under it."

But another underwater archaeologist feels that the two pro-
fessions are not only compatible, but that they benefit each other.
To prove his point, thirty-six-year-old underwater archaeologist
C. Duncan Mathewson is actively combining underwater archaeology with treasure hunting and coming up with some remarkable

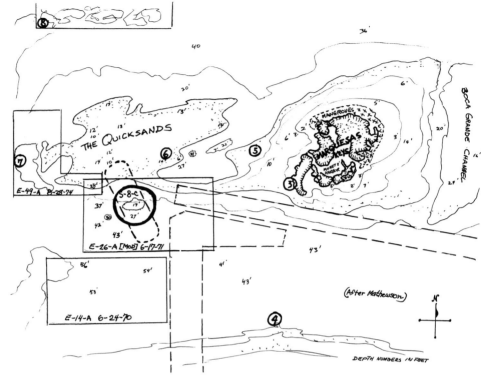

The Atocha wreck site is located on a tongue of the continental shelf which projects westward from the Marquesas Keys towards the Dry Tortugas. The site is situated on the edge of shallow shoals known as the "Quicksands" and is completely out of sight of land. The nearest point of land is the Marquesas Keys some nine and a half nautical miles to the east. The site is listed as 8MO141 in the State archaeological file and designated on this chart by the cigar-shaped figure outlined by the broken line aligned NW-SE. The area which was under the salvage contract (S-8C) with the State of Florida is indicated by the solid circle. The rectangular areas on the chart indicate the official areas covered by magnetometer surveys in the search for the Atocha and her sister ship the Margarita. The solid lines indicate the areas searched by Treasure Salvors, Inc., while the dotted lines indicate the areas magged by competitors. The numbered circles represent the successive positioning of the Theodolite tower for maintaining precise locational data on the anomalies encountered during the magnetometer surveys conducted by Treasure Salvors, Inc. (Courtesy Duncan Mathewson)

results—not too surprising when one considers the young man's academic background. Duncan did his undergraduate work at Dartmouth College and he worked on his Ph.D. dissertation at the Institute of Archaeology, University of London. In 1964 he went to West Africa to serve as a research archaeologist for the Ghanaian government and the University of Ghana. Moving on to Jamaica in 1971, he was appointed government archaeologist for the Institute of Jamaica. In 1973 he returned to the United States, where he became an archaeological consultant working for Treasure Salvors, Inc., to develop underwater methodology and research procedures for the recovery of archaeological data from the site being worked off Key West.

This interview took place in the lounge of the Eastern Airways terminal at Miami International Airport. Duncan, about six feet tall, with longish blond hair, a small neatly trimmed beard and wearing glasses, came prepared for the interview with rolled-up field charts showing the search site and position of finds in the area near the Marquesas. He came across as a sincere, dedicated individual, very open and sharing with his information. Words came easy to him; the right word seemed always on the tip of his tongue. (He knows his work well and is obviously very good at it.) At the end of the interview he mentioned plans to remain with the *Atocha* project until all the finds are made. Then he would like to go into teaching, preferably in the field of underwater archaeology.

Duncan, my interviews with Mel Fisher and other members of Treasure Salvors have carried us through the period involving the discovery of the silver bars from the Atocha. *Could you pick up the story from there and tell us what your archaeological findings indicate about the whereabouts of the main body of the wreck?*

Yes. After finding about six thousand coins and the three silver ingots in the area known as the Bank of Spain, about nine and a half nautical miles from the Marquesas, it was obvious that this was a major point of impact of at least part of a vessel. Now, one of my major jobs was to establish good archaeological control so that we could map the site and obtain as good an archaeological provenience as possible to develop hypotheses from which we could theorize about where the major part of the ship lay.

Since we had only found some sixty to eighty tons of ballast, this left about one hundred to one hundred fifty tons yet to be found. Therefore, I was convinced that we were only working part of the vessel. Continued work along the main northwest-southeast axis showed us that this assumption was correct. Very little pottery was recovered, very little rigging, no ship structure, and the ballast content was not enough to suggest a complete ship.

We got indications that we were dealing with the sterncastle. We found armaments, navigation instruments, and other items that would have been carried in this part of the ship. As we developed our search patterns along the main axis of the site running for about three hundred thirty meters from the galleon anchor to the edge of the sand, we began to pick up more evidence to suggest that this was a secondary dispersal, and not the primary ballast deposits where we would find the heavy ordnance, perhaps several of the anchors, the large majority of the rigging, the ceramics, and, of course, the main heavy cargo and treasure where the ship settled in, rather than where it was dispersed.

So we continued our search patterns along the main axis utilizing surface control buoys as well as bottom cables to establish good control on the bottom as well as on the surface. We continued doing this type of recovery throughout 1973 and 1974. At the beginning of this dive season in 1975 we developed an alternative theory, that it may be to the northwest of the galleon anchor, but after a systematic digging in this area and the recording of archaeological data stratigraphically as well as horizontally, it became very evident that we were dealing with the tailing off of the cultural deposits.

You mention the galleon anchor. Could you tell us about that?

Yes. The first indication that there was a site in this area of the Quicksands came from the location of the galleon anchor through the magnetometer survey conducted by Bob Holloway. The finding of the galleon anchor occurred on the third pass in

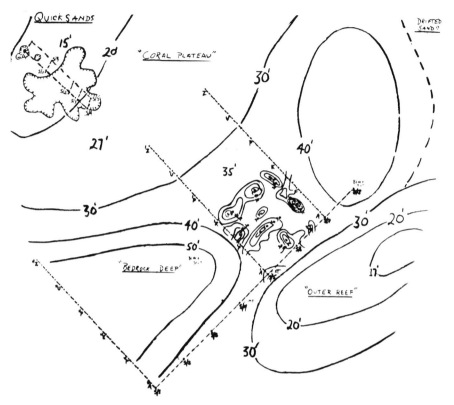

The hatched areas in the "Quicksand" part of the site indicate the parts of the Galleon Anchor grid which were dug prior to the 1975 digging season. The large grid in the southeast part of the site was laid to establish close horizontal control for an intra-site magnetometer survey which would pick up ferrous material associated with the primary cultural deposits. Localized patterns of magnetic anomalies represented on this map by intensity contour intervals indicate some ferrous material spread out in the Southeast Corridor between the "Outer Reef" and the "Coral Plateau." It is believed that some of these patterns represent shipwreck material stemming from the sinking of the Atocha in about fifty feet of water some two hundred to three hundred meters inside the "Outer Reef." Work is now under way to redefine these magnetic anomalies and to determine their orientation in relation to the nine bronze cannon recently found nearby in the Southeast Corridor in about 42 feet of water. (Courtesy Duncan Mathewson)

this area. That is to say, the first two surveys done there did not pick up the anchor, and it was only on the third try that Holloway was able to register a double ping, which indicated a very large iron mass that turned out to be the galleon anchor. Soon after finding it several things were recovered in the immediate vicinity. Don Kincaid was very much involved with this part of the operation, finding several pieces of gold chain. Coins, mini-balls, some ballast were all recovered there, and this led Treasure Salvors to believe that they had located one of the main galleons of the 1622

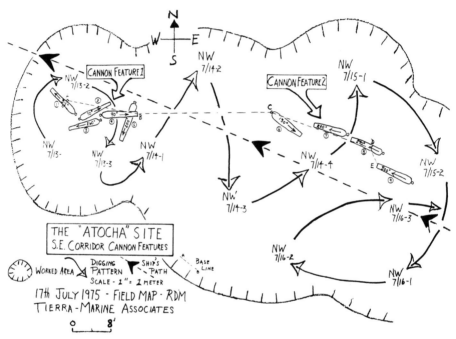

This field map drawn by archaeologist Duncan Mathewson tells a story in itself. From the position of the cannons he was able to determine which way the shipwreck was going. Cannon No. 4 in Feature 1 is the so-called "shark cannon" with its muzzle worn by sea turtles. Interestingly, the bronze cannons failed to show up on magging surveys because the magnetometer only records disturbances in the earth's magnetic field caused by deposits of iron. (Courtesy Duncan Mathewson)

Archaeologist Duncan Mathewson's astute observations of shipwreck clues are providing information that may lead treasure hunters to the final resting place of the main treasure load of the Atocha.

flota, which at that time they believed to be the *Margarita*.

But finding the three silver bars suggested that the ship was indeed the *Atocha*. The galleon anchor is slightly over five meters long and has an internal ring diameter of thirty-four inches. It is definitely galleon size. It is also definitely aligned on the main configuration spread of cultural material, and the ballast and all the shipwreck material is definitely associated with it. The anchor has served as the archaeological datum point, from which we have set out the bottom cable system and the surface control buoys demarking the whole galleon anchor corridor into three distinct archaeological units.

In checking out the area to the northwest of the anchor and finding the cultural material tailing off, did that start you looking in the opposite direction?

Yes. This evidence ruled out the northwest hypothesis and confirmed my earlier theory that the main lode was to be found slightly out in water about fifty or fifty-feet deep in the south-west corridor.

In order to test this hypothesis in 1974, we set out a mag grid from which we established good control in a magnetometer survey. This survey revealed a large number of magnetic disturbances, suggesting once again that this was a primary area in which we could concentrate our search.

Early in the spring of 1975 we developed a sub-bottom profile survey and a side-scanning survey off the *Easy Living* that produced a number of very interesting anomalies that we planned to follow up with a visual search. This was one of the things that led Dirk Fisher to find the first group of cannon on the thirteenth of July.

Could you describe what Dirk saw when he found that first cannon feature?

Right. Dirk perhaps believed in the deepwater hypothesis more than anybody in the company, and he was primarily interested in that deep area. So, it was one of our sub-bottom profile features that led him out there in the *Northwind* to check it out.

Kane and Dirk Fisher show items recovered from the shipwreck site near Marquesas Keys. The coins and silver candlestick held by Kane (left) are heavily sulphided while the gold ingot in Dirk's hand remains as clean as the day it was poured.

Treasure Salvor's ill-fated salvage boat Northwind *on station off the Marquesas searching for the* Atocha. *The vessel took on water at night, turned turtle and claimed the lives of three people, including Dirk and Angel Fisher.*

Anchoring over an anomaly he started digging down to it with a water jet. He was down four or five feet, doing a good job of cutting through the mud, when the *Northwind* dragged anchor, moving slightly to the east.

The next morning Dirk swam out to reset the anchor when he found the five bronze cannon. They all lay in a close group fully exposed on the bottom. One was very eroded along the muzzle and evidently this eroding had been going on for some time. We learned that there was a loggerhead turtle in the area and that this was in fact a "turtle roost." Confirmation came when we went to lift this particular cannon which we called the "shark cannon" because of the configuration of the erosion on the muzzle. The turtle was there and we lifted him aboard at the same time we brought up the cannon. So this has probably been a turtle roost for quite some time, perhaps as long as the cannon have been there.

Was that the only cannon worn that way?

Some of the others were worn in different ways. This cannon

in particular was heavily worn from the muzzle down to underneath the chase. And this, I believe, was what the turtle was coming under. The muzzle of this cannon was resting atop another so that it was elevated. It enabled the turtle to follow right along the main axis of the tube. Some of the other cannon had erosion around the cascabels, the dolphins, and the trunnions.

After Dirk located these cannon, he set up over the feature and began working systematically around it to determine what was associated with the cannon and, of course, to see whether or not there was a lot of ballast and perhaps other cannon. And some distance away, a few days later, he did indeed come upon what we call Cannon Feature Two, four more bronze cannon buried beneath about two feet of sand. Because they were protected by the surrounding substrate, these tubes were in better condition than those in the first group.

Have the cannon provided you with any new information about the wreck?

Yes, indeed. The positions of the cannon themselves indicate that part of the structure that deposited them came from somewhere east-southeast, along a bearing of one hundred twenty degrees. The present hypothesis suggests that these cannon represent the armaments from the upper deck, which sheared off from the main lower part of the vessel together with the sterncastle. This part, which probably broke off during the second hurricane, drifted slowly toward the northwest, depositing the first group of cannon in the Cannon Feature Two with one roll, and with another roll the cannon came off the other side of the vessel and were deposited in the configuration we have in Cannon Feature One. Interestingly, the distance between the first cannon feature and the second cannon feature is about the same distance as the beam of the vessel, about thirty feet.

The two most important things about the cannon were their directions and the nature of the distance between the first and second features. Taking measurements and estimating the weights of the cannon indicated that we were dealing with upper rather than lower deck armament. The orientation of the cannon and their relative positions, one to another and one feature to another feature, told me that one feature represented one roll of the vessel, dumping the armaments and the second feature represented the other side of the armaments coming off.

Now, when that wreckage lost about fifteen tons, which those cannon represent, it became far more buoyant and therefore more affected by the tides and the currents. Also, I suspect that there was a slight change of direction just after the last loss of cannon, because the first cannon in Cannon Feature One has the identical bearing of the Bank of Spain main axis with that of the galleon anchor, three hundred fifteen degrees. It therefore suggests that this part of the structure was torn off the main hull. It dumped its upper armament, there was a slight change of direction, and it went right on in to the Bank of Spain area where that part of the vessel broke up, spreading its guts, continuing out to the northwest until which time it peters out.

So we've really got three main parts of the site: one, where she hit on the outer reef, breached her hull, then went on to sink in that deeper area of about fifty to fifty-five feet. We know she was intact when she went down because the documentation tells us that the mizzenmast was erect, the hatches were secure, the deck was secure, so we are dealing here with a vessel that more or less sank still intact.

It was the second hurricane that broke her up and sheared off her upper deck, sheared off the sterncastle, and sent that part of the vessel in toward the shallow area where she dumped her cannon and continued on into the shallow area. So our concern now is to start out from our known position, which is the end, Cannon Feature Two, and work our systematic search along the main axis, which should lead us along a corridor where we will find more and perhaps bigger ballast as we go, until eventually we will come upon the area where the ship originally sank. And it is there that we are going to find the primary ballast deposits, and these are going to be much different. There will be structure, a great accumulation of cargo and rigging, of artifacts, personal effects, bullion. The whole thing is going to be entirely different from what we've got up here in the shallow area, which was secondary scatter.

Diving to set a dragged anchor, Dirk Fisher discovered bronze cannons once belonging to the Atocha. These two were brought up. Note the amount of abrasion on the cannon muzzle to the left.

So we will be concentrating on locating and archaeologically defining the parameters of the primary ballast deposits at which time we are going to be systematically recording and mapping this area before we begin to bring up any of the artifacts found to be associated with it. I suspect that most of the deposits will be down in the mud, but I don't anticipate that we are going to have to dig too deep. This mud is the same type as that forming in Florida Bay, and we know that is being deposited very slowly. It is forming on top of the same type of bedrock, Key Largo limestone, and under the same general conditions. So with the slow forming mud here, the historical material should therefore be in the top three or four feet. We will not have to go all the way down to bedrock, about twelve feet below the mud. It's only a matter of going three or four feet into the mud. We will be working on these ballast deposits with a water jet and air lift and using a two meter open grid system on top of the ballast deposits, trying to recover as much data on the artifact proveniences as possible.

Thank you, Duncan.

Unfortunately, there is a tragic postscript to the story of the bronze cannon. Prior to their discovery, Mel Fisher told his Treasure Salvor divers that he would give $10,000 to the first person to find a bronze cannon (valued today at $20,000 apiece, according to Fisher). When his own son, twenty-one-year-old Dirk Fisher, made the find, Mel happily presented him and his attractive wife, Angel, with a check for the promised reward. The young couple hurried to Miami to buy a Peugeot sports car with the money. "Boy, they were on top of the world," said Mel. Then it was back to work aboard the *Northwind* at the wreck site.

After recovering a couple of the cannon a week later, Dirk, skipper of the sixty-foot *Northwind*, finished up the day as usual

Both bronze muzzles were alike. Sea turtles rubbing their shells against the further cannon caused the odd shape which the treasure hunters quickly dubbed the "shark cannon."

by moving the rust-stained converted tugboat to its nightly anchorage seven miles to the leeward of the Marquesas. Besides Dirk and Angel, who shared an inside air-conditioned cabin, nine other crew members were aboard: four divers asleep in the crew's quarters forward and five others asleep topside. Among the latter was the company's underwater photographer, Don Kincaid.

Sometime in the predawn hours of July 19, Kincaid awakened with a start. Sensing something wrong he got up from where he was sleeping in the wheelhouse and looked around. The *Northwind* was listing badly. A toilet fitting had failed; seawater was pouring into the bilge. Kincaid hurried below and found water knee-deep in the engine room. Awakened about the same time, the expedition's chief mechanic, Donnie Jonas, joined Kincaid in the engine room. The two tried unsuccessfully to correct the list by pushing machinery to the high side of the vessel. Unknown to either, a fuel transfer valve was also apparently defective, allowing fuel from the port tank to pour across to the starboard tank, rapidly increasing the list.

While Jonas worked with the bilge pump, Kincaid raced topside to alert the others. Seconds later the vessel rolled over and turned turtle. The last thing Kincaid saw before he was hurled overboard was his lighted flashlight being sucked down through the engine room hatch in an angry rush of water.

Six divers were spilled into the sea; two others managed to swim free of the overturned hulk. Trapped suddenly in the watery black chaos of the engine room, Jonas glimpsed a light. Struggling toward it he grasped Kincaid's flashlight. With it he made his way to an air pocket, then swam out the hatch and came up. Fifteen minutes later the *Northwind* sank.

Twenty-one-year-old diver Rick Gage did not get out. Neither did Dirk nor Angel Fisher. They were brought up the next day. Gage had made it as far as a porthole but was unable to go farther. Dirk was still in his cabin. A head wound indicated that he was probably knocked unconscious. Angel Fisher came the closest to swimming free of the wreck. In the flooded compartment she had apparently managed to swim through the tangled rope and gear-laden passageway to a hatch, but in the dark confusion of the overturned vessel, she failed to realize that to get out she had to swim down rather than up.

The survivors, in life jackets and on rafts, were picked up shortly after 8:00 A.M. that morning by another Treasure Salvors' boat that had anchored in the area for the night.

"It's a powerful ocean. It takes men and ships," said a distraught Mel Fisher. But even as the funerals took place, another vessel with fresh divers was sent back to the *Atocha* site. "Dirk would have wanted us to go on," said Fisher.

Index

239